Souped Up

THIS IS A CARLTON BOOK

Text and design copyright © 1999 Carlton Books Limited

This edition published by Carlton Books Limited 2000
20 Mortimer Street
London
W1N 7RD
www.carltonbooks.com

CIP data for this book is available on request from the publisher

ISBN 1 84222 0055

Executive Editor: Sarah Larter
Art Editor: Tim Brown
Design: blu inc
Picture Research: Sarah Moule
Production: Garry Lewis
Original Photography: Howard Shooter

Printed and bound in Spain by
Gráficas Estella, S. A. Navarra.

Souped Up

The Gourmet's Guide
With over 70 wholesome,
hearty, and healthy recipes

JANE PETTIGREW

CARLTON

CONTENTS

INTRODUCTION

I once read in a book on English cookery, published, I think, some time in the 1920s, "A woman who cannot make soup should not be allowed to marry"! Well, that may have been said with tongue in cheek but thank goodness the kinds of attitude that tied women to the kitchen sink, valued them only for the quality of their soup, and assumed that men had no place at the stove have long gone.

Opposite: Wholesome soups have provided essential nourishment around the globe for thousands of years.

Nowadays, too few people cook at all. Ready-made meals and convenience foods are steadily turning us into a nation of microwave-operatives, and "cooking" involves no more than peeling a layer of tinfoil or plastic wrap from a neat plastic tray, pressing a couple of buttons and standing around waiting for the beeper to indicate that "dinner is ready". Where's the fun in that?

Cooking can be one of the most rewarding of activities. And for those who do not like complicated recipes and long-winded preparations, soup-making is one of the easiest. After all, you don't have to worry about different dishes all having to be ready at the same time. In almost all cases, soup can be made ahead, rarely spoils if guests are late—just switch off and wait, then reheat when they eventually arrive—and doesn't leave a trail of dirty dishes. And it is easy to eat, adapts to all sorts of both sweet and savory ingredients, can be adjusted to the weather's unpredictable behaviour, and is absolutely under your control in terms of what you put into it.

Everyone has a favorite soup. And a favorite soup memory. Remember those childhood bowlfuls of "cream of tomato" or thick rich oxtail? The first time you tried noodle soup in a Chinese restaurant and couldn't quite manage to maneuver the noodles where you thought they ought to be but helplessly watched them slither on and off the spoon while your hunger grew? And the dish of *bouillabaisse* that appeared in front of your eyes on your first teenage trip to France and you couldn't quite believe all those shells and tentacles and bones floating in your bowl?

Soup—often made with whatever cheap ingredients were available—was once a poor person's staple food, and soup kitchens the Victorians' way of offering sustenance to the "underprivileged" in society. Today, things have certainly changed and soup has become the latest trendy food for lunchtime snacking or evening indulgence. Today's recipes dip into exotic flavorings and bring

together unlikely combinations that stop you in your tracks and spark off thoughts of tropical beaches and seafood feasts, cosy fireside suppers and summer picnics.

In 1877, Grimond de la Reynière wrote in his *Book of the Table*, "soup is to dinner what a portico is to a palace, or an overture to an opera", and that may well have been true in those days. But today, soup is playing a far more important role than simply as a hint of things to come later in the meal. As an appetizer, a sumptuous soup can claim its place as a major part of an entire meal, and a chunky soup full of different colors and textures and brimming with goodness actually is the entire meal. Consommés, broths, or bisques can still be modest in-between canapés at posh dinners or banquets. And thick wholesome soups, potages, and chowders also fit into the lunchtime or snack menu and are becoming a major feature in the modern high street soup bar as a truly healthy alternative to burger and chips or a simple sandwich. After all, why fill up with fatty unhealthy foods when a mug of piping hot—or chilled in summer—soup satisfies all your hunger pangs as well as your body's basic need for nourishment and energy.

Opposite and Left: A staple food wherever you are in the world.
Above: One of today's trendy soup bars.

CHAPTER ONE

FOR GOODNESS' SAKE

Soup has a long and respectable pedigree. Apparently the ancient Greeks and Romans favored it as an everyday food, not just for the poorer members of society but as a staple for the ruling classes. The first recorded recipe from Rome was for a gruel made from a mixture of barley pounded with other toasted cereals and cooked in water to make something called *potus*—a kind of liquid food, named from the Latin *potare* to drink.

Opposite: *Madonna and Child with Gruel* c. 1450 Gerard David.

The Greeks made a similar porridge, called *alphiton*, from barley flour, linseed meal, coriander seed, salt, and water, thickened with a little millet and sometimes with lamb or chicken juices added for flavor.

In China over a thousand years ago, the imperial household served soups of beef with sour plums, or salted fish with venison and bamboo shoots, or beef with dog and turnip, as an everyday part of meals. Only soups containing meat were considered acceptable as offerings for visitors in such an eminent establishment, while the peasants brewed up stew-like soups of grains and vegetables. By the sixth century AD, Chinese recipes included goat, pork, rice, fermented bean paste, and ginger.

Soups in Europe

European cookery derived largely from classical Roman cuisine and so the oat- and grain-based gruels familiar to the ancient Romans (and Greeks) also featured in the European diet. Pagan mid-winter festivities held in honour of Dagda, Celtic god of plenty, featured a runny porridge of cornmeal, meat and fruits of which generous quantities were boiled up as a symbol of the abundance and plenty that would eventually return in the spring.

In Britain, that sloppy mess of winter nourishment gradually transformed itself into Christmas plum pudding with the addition of spices and dried fruits, breadcrumbs and sugar, but it started as a soup.

In fourteenth-century England, during Richard II's reign, a porridge of boiled ground wheat, milk, and saffron was served with venison at court, while poorer folk ate a mush of dried peas boiled in bacon stock. And while the wealthy lords and ladies ate their boiled meats at the high table, the servants dipped hunks of bread—called soppes, sops, sippets, or trenchers—into the juices and stocks the meats had been stewed in.

From those early gruels developed all manner of *potages, pots au feu,* and *soppes,* the basic ingredients becoming more exciting and appetizing with the addition of meat scraps, stocks, and juices left over from the stewing process. By the fifteenth century, soup was being

served as a food in its own right as an acceptable dish in any household.

In Britain, soup really came into its own in Victorian times when the serving of food radically changed due to an increased interest in European styles of eating. Prior to the mid-nineteenth century, British meal tables were laden with all sorts of dishes, mainly of meat, all at the same time and guests ate at random from platters of roast, stewed, boiled, and fricasséed poultry, tongue, fish, game, beef, and other meats.

During Queen Victoria's long reign, a new interest in French cooking brought with it the idea of serving the dishes as separate courses, and so menus offered soup, then fish, then an entrée, and finally a sweet or dessert. The first two courses were often placed on the table at the same time, with the soup or roast meat in the middle and *hors d'oeuvres* placed around the outside of the

Above: Pottery figure depicting a Roman banquet.
Above right: A medieval German image of a kitchen scene.

Opposite: A dreary Victorian soup kitchen.
Overleaf: A a grand banqueting scene from fifteenth century England.

table—the term referring in those days to the position of the smaller side dishes on the table rather than to their place on the menu.

The fashion for French cuisine also introduced new words for soup into the English language and fashionable hosts and hostesses started serving *consommé* or *velouté* instead of just "soup".

A New Direction

Isabella Beeton, Britain's best-known cookery writer of the nineteenth century, wrote in 1861 in her *Book of Household Management*:

It has been asserted that English cookery is, nationally speaking, far from being the best in the world. More than this, we have frequently been told by brilliant foreign writers, half philosophers, half chefs, that we are the worst cooks on the face of the earth … We are glad to note, however, that soups of vegetables, fish, meat and game, are now very frequently found in the homes of the English middle classes, as well as in the mansions of the wealthier and more aristocratic; and we take this to be one evidence that we are on the right road to an improvement in our system of cookery.

To emphasize the point, Mrs Beeton included in her book fifty pages of stocks and soups with names like "Soup à la Flamande" (a mix of asparagus and root vegetables), "Kale Brose" (ox-head and cow-heel), "Soup Maigre" (without meat), and "Prince of Wales's Soup" (turnips in veal stock).

Her *Useful Soup for Benevolent Purposes* was

… used in the winter of 1858 by the Editress [that is, Isabella herself] for distribution amongst about a dozen families of the village near where she lives … She has reason to believe that the soup was very much liked, and gave, to the members of those families, a dish of warm comforting food.

Isabella Beeton was not the first or the only Victorian to commend soup as a nourishing food for the poor. Soup kitchens and the distribution of cheap soups to those in need were features of nineteenth-century life and offered not just nutrition but also shelter. As one benevolent society explained in 1811, "the soup kitchen provides an important focal point for the development of social contact and human interaction to meet basic needs of sociability". The human need for a social network was met, and so, too, were the body's requirements for nourishment. By serving vegetables, herbs, and grains with the water or stock in which they were boiled, none of the goodness was lost and so a greater benefit was derived from the gruels and broths made available by the charitable institutions.

The Perfect Nourishment

It is the fact that home-made soups lose none of the goodness of their ingredients that has given them their role as restoratives and tonics and as easily digested nourishment for the invalid or convalescent. In China, chicken soups were traditionally given after childbirth to help the new mother regain her strength, while rice gruels with salt and ginger were fed to invalids for their health-promoting properties. In Europe, beef tea, made by gently infusing beef in hot water for several hours to extract all the goodness from the meat, was a standard food for the sick.

As it demands none of the effort involved in chewing, is easily digested and readily absorbed into the system, soup was and still is the perfect food for such situations. This, as one Victorian food writer explained, actually led to some people refusing to eat soup "as a weak wash fit only for babies and invalids". And it was perhaps for this reason that Dr Hoffman's fictional Augustus turned against his daily bowlful in *Struwwelpeter*, written in 1844:

Augustus was a chubby lad
Fat ruddy cheeks Augustus had.
And everybody saw with joy
The plump and hearty, healthy boy.
He ate and drank as he was told
And never let his soup get cold.
But one day, one cold winter's day,
He screamed out "Take the soup away!
O take the nasty soup away!
I won't have any soup today."

The poem continues through the week with Augustus steadfastly refusing to drink his soup and growing daily thinner and thinner. Eventually, readers were told to study the illustration beside the poem and take note:

Look at him now, the fourth day's come!
He scarcely weighs a sugar plum;
He's like a little bit of thread,
And on the fifth day, he was dead!

Poor Augustus. Perhaps he had simply had too many people pestering him to eat his soup and treating him like a baby.

But there is no doubt that all the reasons which make soup an excellent invalid food also make it an undisputed

Above: An American advertisement for clam broth.
Opposite left: Illustration from Mrs Beeton's esteemed tome c.1861.

source of nourishment for all of us. I don't mean the packet soups and tinned varieties to which all sorts of sugars, monosodium glutamate, colorants. and flavorings have been added. Those were developed in the 1940s and 50s as convenience foods and for a while took over from "proper" home-made soups in many kitchens. But in the last ten years or so, there has been a growing demand for soups that are fresher, healthier, tastier, purer, and more nutritious than those funny, glutinous mixtures that come out of tins.

And as more and more of us worry about what has actually gone into the pre-packed food we buy, home-made soups are obviously the answer. It means we can buy exactly what we like, have total control over the ingredients, cook them for as long or as short a time as we choose. And with the right equipment, even lack of time cannot be an excuse for not making your own, for most soup recipes are really quick and easy to make.

Soup today is an exciting gourmet food that suits our fast-paced lives. Nourishing, satisfying, comforting, stylish, easy to prepare, and easy to eat—soup can be whatever you want it to be for almost any occasion.

CHAPTER TWO

THE SOUP KITCHEN

It is a myth that soup can be made from whatever leftovers you happen to have in your refrigerator or larder. Making soup is no different from preparing any other kind of dish. Although stocks can be made by boiling bones and carcasses that have been stripped of all their meat, and perhaps the odd carrot or stick of celery that has lain in the refrigerator for several days, a good soup really does have to be made with fresh, carefully selected ingredients. But you also need to have a good range of seasonings, sauces, flours, grains, pulses, and seeds in the larder ready to add to whatever fresh vegetables, fish, meats, and fruits that will form the basis of the soup. This chapter lists of the basic ingredients most frequently used in soups. It is very helpful to have these always in stock.

Herbs

Basil

Does not hold its superb flavor well when dried, so is best used fresh; in a grow pot, as sold by some supermarkets, the herb will go on growing in the kitchen as long as it is well watered.

Bay leaves

Powerful aromatic flavoring; use sparingly.

Bouquet Garni

Use ready-made sachets or fresh herbs tied together or put in a cheesecloth bag. Basic bouquet garni herbs include parsley, thyme, and a bay leaf, but others may be added as you choose.

Chervil

Mild, sweet, and aromatic, chervil is good in chicken and vegetable stocks and broths.

Curry leaves

Dried curry leaves add a hint of spicy sweetness to stocks and soups.

Above: Add fresh herb to soups to suit your taste.

Dill

Use fresh in fish soups and stocks and for garnishing; particularly good with salmon.

Fennel

The fresh vegetable is extremely useful in stocks; the seeds are good in fish stocks.

Garlic

An absolute essential in all stocks and soups; use fresh garlic or squeeze a little from a tube of garlic paste.

Ginger

Fresh root ginger gives oriental and Asian-style soups their characteristic pungency; keep in the refrigerator.

Lemon Grass

Adds a wonderful delicate lemony flavor, so familiar in Thai and Chinese cooking; chop small or bruise a stalk and infuse in stocks and soups; keep in the refrigerator.

Above: Garlic adds vital vitamins as well as flavor.
Opposite: A traditional herb garden full of scents and flavors.

Marjoram

A lovely sweet flavor; excellent in all vegetable and meat stocks and soups.

Mint

Powerful herb excellent in small quantities with lamb and with cucumber, apple, and melon; best used fresh.

Mixed Dried Herbs

Useful if fresh herbs are not available; dried herbs are always more concentrated in flavor, so use sparingly.

Oregano

Similar to marjoram, adds a lovely sweet flavor to any stock or soup.

Parsley

Essential to all stocks, and useful for adding just before serving soups and for garnishing.

Peppercorns

Add to all stocks and include in bouquets garnis. Of all the different colors, black peppercorns add the best flavor.

Rosemary

Very powerful flavor so use with care in lamb soups or in bouquets garnis.

Sage

Powerful herb that goes well with pork and ham; use with care.

Tarragon

Wonderful with mushrooms and other vegetables or fish; use sparingly.

Thyme

One of the most useful of garden herbs; adds interest to almost any dish and lifts a dull flavor to something special.

Above: Fresh herbs will add depth to your soups.
Left: Black peppercorns add a lively flavor.

Spices

Caraway Seeds

A tasty addition to soups made with pork or lamb.

Cardamom

Add the seeds to Asian-style soups that include coconut cream, cilantro, and cumin.

Ground Cilantro

Good with fish, chicken, and any vegetable soups.

Cinnamon

Use with pork and lamb dishes.

Cumin

Blends well with the flavor of coconut cream and adds pungency to Asian-style soups.

Nutmeg

Turmeric

Adds a pleasant musky flavor to Asian-style vegetables soups, but is quite powerful, so use sparingly.

Use with broccoli, zucchini, and root vegetables; or shake a little over a soup as a garnish.

Above: Ground turmeric.
Left: Add freshly grated nutmeg for a sweet spiciness.

Sauces and Oils

Anchovy Sauce

Useful for adding character to fish stocks and soups.

Chili Sauce/Hot Pepper Sauce

Use with great care (start with just 2–3 drops and then add more if required) to spice up a stock or soup that is a little lifeless.

Coconut Cream

Available in cartons and tins; adds the creamy sweetness found in Thai and other Asian cuisines.

Consommé

Keep a can or two of beef or fish consommé in the cupboard for those days when you do not have the time or inclination to make your own.

Fish sauce

Add a few drops to strengthen the flavor of fish soups.

Above: White crunchy coconut flesh.
Right: Use olive oil instead of other oils or butters.

Garlic Paste

Use instead of fresh garlic; very concentrated so use sparingly.

Olive Oil

Much better for sautéeing and frying than sunflower or other oils (it oxidizes less easily with heat than other oils and therefore releases fewer "free radicals" that damage body cells); for general use, choose a light variety, for richer flavored soups choose a darker, richer virgin olive oil.

Madeira

Like sherry, adds a rich, sweet subtlety to vegetable or chicken blends.

Mirin

Japanese sweet rice wine, adds a sherry-like flavor to soups.

Miso

Fermented soybean paste, comes in different types and different colors, that are either salty or sweet; combines well with vegetables, white meat, and fish.

Pesto

Extremely useful to add that lovely flavor of basil, parmesan cheese, and pine nuts; stir into soups or spoon a little in as a garnish; or use to spread on bread that is going to be turned into croûtons.

Sherry

Add to Chinese or Japanese-style thin soups to give a subtle sweetness; also good with some thick soups, particularly zucchini and broccoli.

Soy Sauce

Gives a salty depth to Chinese-style mixtures; use carefully, remembering that the darker ones are saltier and thicker.

Tabasco Sauce

Use with care as it is very hot; useful for spicing up a flat-tasting soup.

Tomato Purée

Good for thickening and concentrating flavor in vegetable and meat soups.

Worcester Sauce

Add a few drops to give a peppery, spicy flavor to beef, lamb or pork soups.

Above: Spicy, peppery Tabasco sauce.
Right: Tomato sauce or purée is a useful staple ingredient to have in your store cupboard.

Thickening Agents

Arrowroot

Thickens without making the liquid go as cloudy as other flours; blend with cold water before adding to the soup.

Cornstarch

Gives a clearer, lighter consistency than wheat flour and needs blending thoroughly with cold milk or water before being added to the soup or stock; 2 teaspoons have the same thickening power as 1 tablespoon of wheat flour.

Flour (plain wheat)

The most commonly used flour for thickening sauces and soups; mix with a little cold milk or water before adding to the soup or work into softened butter to make a *beurre manié* (see p.54).

Kuzu

The Japanese equivalent of arrowroot; mix with a little cold water before adding to the soup or broth.

Potato Flour

Use in the same way as rice flour or cornstarch; 1 teaspoon has the same thickening power as 1 tablespoon of wheat flour.

Rice Flour

Useful for thickening; should not go lumpy, but mix with a little cold milk or water before adding, just in case; 2 teaspoons have the same thickening power as 1 tablespoon of wheat flour.

Above: Wheat flour.

Nuts, Seeds, and Grains

Barley

Good for adding bulk and extra nourishment; needs soaking or boiling before adding to soups; takes about $1^{1}/_{2}$ hours in total to cook.

Beans

Add any kind of bean to soups, such as cannellini, navy, kidney, borlotti, adzuki, and black beans; most dried beans need soaking overnight in plenty of cold water before draining and rinsing ready for use; alternatively, buy cans of beans and drain and rinse them well before adding to the soup mixture.

Lentils

For chunky soups use small green puy lentils, which do not fall apart but keep their firmness and nutty texture, or use larger green or brown lentils; orange lentils break down quickly when boiled, so are better used in soups that are to be puréed.

Nuts

Add ground hazelnuts or almonds to thicken soups and add a nutty sweetness to the flavor; or use chopped toasted hazelnuts or toasted flaked almonds as a garnish.

Oats

Add to thick chunky soups for extra nourishment and texture.

Rice

Adds texture and body to thinner soups; good in vegetable and chicken mixtures.

Seeds

Toasted sesame seeds, sunflower seeds, and pumpkin seeds are the best in terms of nutritional value and flavor; add to the soup or use as a garnish.

See "Final Touches" (pp.114–25) for other ideas for garnishes.

Above: Beans and pulses add protein and bulk to soups.
Left: Use ground or chopped nuts to give an unusual extra flavor.

Well Equipped

Most kitchens have the basic soup-making pots and pans, blenders and sieves but there are other pieces of equipment which make things a little easier and the soups more successful. Among the most useful kitchen items for soup-making are:

Baking Tray

For cooking croûtons and crostini in the oven.

Blender

A blender gives a smoother texture than a food processor

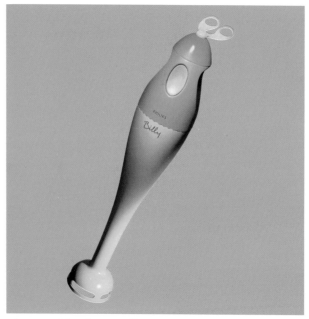

when puréeing "creamed" soups.

Cheesecloth

Have plenty to hand because it is essential for straining stocks and consommé so that no bits of bone, herb or vegetables get left in the liquid.

Chopping Boards

Have several for different purposes and keep one just for onions and garlic; choose wood or melamine.

Colander

For draining beans, vegetables, etc and for lining with cheesecloth to strain stocks and consommés.

Food Processor

When buying consider the capacity; if you are going to be making a lot of soup, choose one that can process large quantities at a time; also consider how easy it is to fill, wash and store.

Funnel

For bottling soups or stocks into bottles for storing in the freezer (rinsed-out plastic milk and juice bottles are very useful here).

Garlic Press

Although it is really easy to chop or mash garlic, some people prefer to squish the garlic cloves in a garlic press; remember, though, they are difficult to clean afterwards and a lot of the garlic flesh is lost.

Grater

For grating root ginger, beets, cheese, and other foods.

Left: A hand-held electric blender.
Above: A food processor is an extremely useful implement for soup cooking.
Opposite: Have a selection of different sized pots and pans at the ready.

Knives

Have a selection of sharp knives for cutting and chopping, a couple of small ones for paring, and a large one with a serrated blade for cutting through big tough vegetables such as pumpkins.

Ladles

Large and generous is the key.

Measuring Jugs

You need at least one that holds 1 quart and that pours well.

Measuring Spoons

For measuring spices, herbs, and thickeners.

Metal Simmer Mat

Useful for controlling the heat underneath a simmering pot.

Above: An array of different knives.

Mixing Bowls

A variety of sizes is useful but have at least one 2 quart bowl for mixing pulverized ingredients from the blender or food processor with other ingredients and liquids.

Mouli-legume

A hand-held vegetable mill useful for pulping potatoes and more stringy vegetables, such as beans and celery.

Nutmeg Grater

Freshly grated nutmeg is much more full of flavor than the ready-grated variety.

Peeler

Choose one that takes off the bare minimum of peel as so much of the goodness in vegetables lies just beneath the skin (whenever you can, simply scrub the skin of carrots, potatoes, etc., rather than remove them altogether).

Rubber Spatulas

For scraping out every last drop from blenders, food processors, and pans.

Saucepans

You need at least one saucepan that will easily hold 3 quarts of liquid: it is much better to have a pan that is too big than to risk having the soup boil over. Side handles make lifting easier and safer; a tight-fitting lid is essential, but it is useful to have ventilation holes in the rim to stop liquids boiling over.

Scrubbing Brush

A hard-bristled one for scrubbing celery and carrots, etc.

Sieves

It is useful to have a couple of different sizes—one fairly large, average meshed sieve which can sit over a bowl to allow stock etc to run through slowly (and which you can easily line with cheesecloth), and one conical, fine-meshed sieve.

Skimming Spoon

Choose a large spoon that is almost flat and can easily be dipped just under the surface of the stock or soup to scoop up oil and fat.

Stockpot

Choose a heavy-bottomed pan that is tall and narrow (to reduce evaporation) and that has a tight-fitting lid; two side handles make lifting easier and safer.

String

For tying up little sachets of cheesecloth that hold herbs for bouquets garnis.

Storage Boxes, Bottles, and Freezer Bags

A stock of different sizes is useful for freezing spare stock and left-over portions of soup.

Wooden Spoons

Have a variety of sizes and shapes.

Whisks

One small and one large for different quantities and different jobs: a big one for whisking thickening agents into large pots of soup and a small one for such tasks as whisking together egg yolks and cream.

Zester

Useful for peeling off neat thin strips of lemon or lime zest for garnishing.

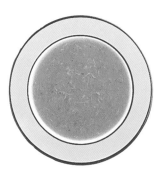

STOCKTAKE

Busy lives today mean that few of us have the time to boil up home-made stocks, and shopping patterns and the increased consumption of ready-made meals means that refrigerators and larders no longer hold meat bones and chicken carcasses that just plead to be thrown into a stock pot to create the base for all sorts of delicious soups. Instead, we have to resort, at worst, to stock cubes (which are too salty and often contain monosodium glutamate), and at best to tins of consommé or ready-made stocks that are available now in most supermarkets and gourmet stores.

eady-made stocks vary considerably in quality, with some being so thin and tasteless that you might as well use water. But the good ones are an excellent alternative and it is a really good idea to keep a pot of each of the different sorts in the freezer. And a good stock really does make a difference to the final taste.

Making Good Stocks

The quality of each stock obviously depends on the ingredients used and on the preparation and handling of what is in the pan. The most important things to remember when making stock are:

- Use a large, tall, and narrow, heavy-bottomed pan that has a tight-fitting lid.
- Trim off as much fat as possible from all meats before putting them into the stockpot.
- Whenever possible, bring meat to the boil and skim off any scum with a wide, flattish spoon before adding vegetables and herbs—scum is much easier to remove when there are no other ingredients in the pan.
- Continue to skim as and when necessary during cooking.
- Cook the stock so slowly that it hardly moves in the pan. Hard boiling causes any fats in the meat to break down so they cannot be removed from the finished stock, so the stock will be cloudy. If necessary, use a heat-diffusing plate over the gas or electric burner to reduce the risk of cooking too fast.
- Do not disturb the contents of the pan while they are simmering.
- At the end of the cooking process, remove as much fat as you possibly can from the stock. Either put layers of folded kitchen paper on top of the liquid after it has settled to absorb the fat or oil, or chill the stock in the refrigerator overnight and then lift the hardened fat off with a knife or spoon.
- If the stock tastes too "thin", reduce it by boiling with the lid off to evaporate some of the water.
- Never over-season at the beginning of the stock-making; it is much better to add more salt and pepper later than end up with a stock that is so salty you cannot use it—if it is only a little too salty, boil a couple of potatoes in it for 15–20 minutes to absorb some of the surplus salt.
- Strain stock through a very fine sieve in order to catch as many of the solids as possible; use wire sieves with an extremely fine mesh, or a colander lined with a double layer of cheesecloth.
- Strain more than once if you feel the stock is not clear enough.
- Never force stock through the sieve, just allow it to run or drip at its own pace.

Dark Stocks

Here are three ways to make a good dark stock:
- Brown the bones, meat trimmings and vegetables in a hot oven (400° F) for 30–40 minutes before adding them to the stockpot.
- Brown a couple of small onions or shallots in their skins in a dry non-stick pan then add them to the stockpot.
- Add a few drops of caramel. Make caramel by slowly melting 1/2 cup sugar until it is a dark golden color, than carefully adding 2/3 cup cold water and boiling until the sugar has dissolved.

Freezing Stocks

Convenient ways to freeze stock include:
- Measure convenient quantities into lidded boxes or freezer containers.
- To freeze soup in plastic bags, place a bag inside a bowl or plastic jug, pour in the soup, seal and leave in the bowl or jug in the freezer until solid enough not to spill.
- Reduce stock quantity by boiling it in an uncovered saucepan until it becomes a thick concentrated liquid which can be frozen in ice cube trays. One cube can then be dissolved in as much water as it needs to turn it back into a tasty stock.

However you store stocks, do not forget to label it, because one stock looks pretty much like any other in its frozen state.

Stock Recipes

Mrs Beeton wrote in 1861, "It is on a good stock, or first good broth and sauce, that excellence in cookery depends … In the proper management of the stock-pot an immense deal of trouble is saved, inasmuch as one stock, in a small dinner, serves all purposes." For those of you who have the time and enjoy starting from scratch so that you have total control over the ingredients you use, here are a few recipes for the most useful and basic stocks. Make them in large quantities, freeze in small amounts and you're all set.

Right: Straining stock through cheesecloth.

Beef Stock

Makes approximately 3 quarts

8lb beef bones, such as ribs, shin, leg,
    pieces of marrow bone
1lb cheap beef (skirt, shin, or flank)
2 carrots, roughly chopped
2 onions, peeled and quartered
2 sticks celery, cut into chunks
1 leek, roughly sliced
5 quarts water
3–4 stalks fresh parsley
3–4 sprigs fresh thyme
2 bay leaves
12–14 black peppercorns
salt to add at the end of the cooking period

1. For a dark stock, preheat the oven to 400° F/200°C. Spread the bones, meat and vegetables in a roasting pan and roast for 30–40 minutes, until browned all over. Place in the stockpot. Drain off the fat or oil from the roasting pan and discard, pour a cup of boiling water into the pan, stir around to mix with all the juices and pour into a stockpot or large saucepan.

2. For a lighter stock, wash the bones under cold running water, then place in the pan with the meat and vegetables.

3. For both dark and light stock, add the water to the pan and slowly bring to the boil. Skim the surface to remove any scum. Add the herbs and peppercorns, reduce the heat, partially cover the pan, and simmer very gently for 3 1/2–4 hours, skimming regularly to remove any scum that rises.

4. Drain the stock through a fine sieve, add a little salt, cool, and chill. Skim off any fat with a flat, wide spoon or leave in the refrigerator until any fat has hardened and can be lifted off.

Chicken Stock

Use as the base for any vegetable or poultry soup or consommé.

Makes approximately 2 1/4 quarts

4 1/2 lb chicken bones, cooked or uncooked,
    plus any giblets and trimmings
3 quarts water
5–6 garlic cloves, skins left on and lightly bruised
4oz mushroom stalks or mushrooms, sliced
2 carrots, scraped and roughly chopped
2 onions, peeled and quartered
2 sticks celery, chopped
1 leek, roughly sliced
3–4 sprigs parsley
3–4 sprigs fresh thyme
2 bay leaves
10 black peppercorns
salt

1. Put the bones and chicken trimmings into a stockpot or large saucepan with the water and bring slowly to the boil. Skim off any scum and add the vegetables, herbs, peppercorns, and a little salt.

2. Bring back to the boil, reduce the heat, and partially cover the pan. Simmer very gently for 2 1/2–3 hours.

3. Strain through a fine sieve, taste, and adjust the seasoning, if necessary, and allow to cool. Mop up any fat from the surface with folded kitchen paper or chill in the refrigerator until any fat has hardened and can be lifted off.

Left: Check the seasoning at the end of the cooking process.

Lamb Stock

To avoid the unpleasant greasiness of lamb fat that can taint the soups, take every scrap of fat from the bones and meat trimmings before you start, and be careful to skim or lift off whatever fat settles on the surface of the stock.

Makes approximately 2 quarts

6½ lb lamb bones (neck, shoulder, breast, etc)
    plus any trimmings of meat, but trimmed of all fat
3 quarts water
2 onions, peeled and quartered
3–4 garlic cloves, skins left on and lightly bruised
2 carrots, scraped and roughly chopped
2oz mushrooms or mushroom stalks, chopped
1 bay leaf
2 sprigs fresh mint
2 sprigs fresh thyme or marjoram

1. Preheat the oven to 400°F/200°C. Put the lamb bones and any meat trimmings into a roasting pan and roast in the oven for 45 minutes, until well browned.

2. Put the bones into a stockpot or large saucepan. Drain off the fat from the roasting pan and discard. Add a cup of boiling water to the roasting pan, stir around to mix with any juices and pour into the stockpot.

3. Add the water to the stockpot, bring slowly to the boil, skim off any scum, then add the vegetables and herbs. Partially cover the pan and simmer very gently for 2½–3 hours. Skim when necessary.

4. Strain the stock through a fine sieve. Taste, and adjust the seasoning, if necessary. Allow to cool. Remove any fat by placing layers of folded kitchen paper on the surface to soak it up, or chill the stock in the refrigerator until any fat has hardened and can be lifted off.

Ham Stock

Ham or bacon stock is particularly good for lentil, pea, and vegetable soups.

Makes approximately 2 quarts

1 ham bone
2 onions, peeled and quartered
2 carrots, scraped and roughly chopped
2 sticks celery, roughly sliced
1 leek, sliced
2 medium potatoes, peeled and roughly chopped
4 stalks fresh parsley
3–4 sprigs fresh thyme
1 bay leaf
6 black peppercorns
2¼ quarts water

1. Put all the ingredients into a stockpot or large saucepan and bring slowly to the boil. Skim as necessary, partially cover the pan, and simmer gently for 3 hours.

2. Strain through a fine sieve and allow to cool. Chill and remove any fat by placing layers of folded kitchen paper on the surface, or allow the stock to chill in the refrigerator until any fat has hardened and can be lifted off.

Right: Meat stock.

Fish Stock

The best fish stocks are made from the bones and trimmings from non-oily fish varieties such as cod, sole, turbot, and halibut. Oily fish such as mackerel, herrings, and sardines are not suitable. Don't simmer for too long as it may make the stock bitter and unpleasant.

Makes 2 quarts

2¼ lb fish bones, heads, and trimmings, plus
    any lobster or shrimp shells saved from
    other dishes
1¼ quarts water
1 cup dry white wine
2 small onions, peeled and roughly chopped
1 carrot, scraped and roughly sliced
1 stick celery, sliced
2 sprigs fresh thyme
3–4 stalks fresh parsley
1 bay leaf
1–2 thick slices fennel
5–6 black peppercorns

1. Wash the fish bones under cold running water, then place in a stockpot or large saucepan with all the other ingredients.

2. Bring slowly to the boil, skim off any scum, partially cover the pan and simmer very gently for 30 minutes.

3. Strain the stock through a very fine sieve, season with a little salt, and cool.

Court Bouillon

This is a very light rather thin stock in which fish is cooked.

Makes approximately 1 quart

1 quart cold water
2 small or 1 medium onion, peeled and roughly
    chopped
1 leek, chopped
2 sticks celery, roughly chopped
2 carrots, scraped and roughly chopped
3 garlic cloves, peeled and roughly chopped
2 thick slices lemon
3–4 black peppercorns
1 bay leaf
2 sprigs fresh parsley
2 sprigs fresh tarragon
¾ cup dry white wine

1. Put all the ingredients into a large saucepan and bring to the boil. Reduce the heat, partially cover, and simmer for 15–20 minutes. Turn off the heat and leave to infuse until completely cold.

2. Strain the stock through a sieve lined with 3–4 layers of wet cheesecloth.

Left: Fish stock.
Above: Court bouillon.

40

Vegetable Stock

Makes approximately 2¼ quarts

2½ quarts water
3 large onions, peeled and roughly chopped
8–10 garlic cloves, skins left on and lightly bruised
4–5 carrots, scraped and roughly sliced
2 leeks, roughly sliced
2 sticks celery, sliced
1 parsnip, peeled and roughly chopped
4–5 stalks fresh parsley
3–4 sprigs fresh thyme
3–4 sprigs fresh marjoram
2 bay leaves
8–10 black peppercorns
salt

1. Place all the ingredients in a stockpot or large saucepan and bring to the boil. Reduce the heat, partially cover the pan, and simmer for 1 hour. Skim off any scum.

2. Strain the stock through a fine sieve and allow to cool.

Below: Use a mixture of fresh vegetables for a flavorsome vegetable stock.

CHAPTER FOUR

PERFECTLY CLEAR

Clear soups and consommés are richly flavored stocks that have been strained to leave no solids in them and then clarified for an even clearer finish. The effect is stylish and light and creates soups that fulfil the traditional role of whetting the appetite and preparing the digestion for what is to follow.

To make clear soups more attractive visually and more interesting to the palate, they are often served with just a few vegetables cut in strips, stars, or cubes, a few slivers of meat or fish, a cushion or two of pasta, a few noodles or miniature gnocchi, a spoonful of rice, half a dozen tiny meatballs—a carefully chosen complement to the crystal-clear liquid.

Any well-made stock can be used as consommé, but the best consommés are "double broths" that have been boiled twice. The first boiling is with water and the raw ingredients for the stock, the second is with the stock from the first boiling and additional ingredients to enrich and concentrate the flavor. And as with the basic stocks, the final quality of the consommé depends on the ingredients used for making both the first stock and the second "double broth".

Clarifying Stock

To clarify a consommé, the stock should have been strained and skimmed very carefully to remove all fat and solids. Then the liquid must be boiled again with a mixture of egg whites and egg shells, which absorb any traces of dissolved solids that have been left behind.

To clarify 1 quart of cold stock, you will need:

1 egg white
1 egg shell, rinsed and crushed
half a small onion, peeled and roughly chopped
1 carrot, scraped and diced small
half a stick of celery, diced
2 ice cubes
1 tablespoon cold water

Mix together the egg white, egg shell, onion, carrot, celery, ice cubes, and cold water and put into a large saucepan with a carefully measured 1 quart of stock.

Bring the pan slowly to the boil, stirring constantly until the contents start boiling. As the stock begins to boil, the egg mixture will form a crust. Stop stirring, reduce the heat and leave to simmer for 20–25 minutes.

Carefully break a hole in the crust without disturbing it more than necessary and with a large ladle, spoon the stock into a fine sieve lined with 3–4 layers of wet cheesecloth.

Do not press the stock through the sieve but allow it to run freely.

Celery Consommé

The light easy flavor of celery is great at the start of a meal and once you have made (or bought) the beef stock, the soup is really simple to make.

Serves 6

1 ¾ quarts beef stock (see p.37), or canned beef consommé
2 heads of celery, chopped (reserving 1 whole stick)
bouquet garni made with 3 sprigs parsley,
    3 sprigs thyme, and a bay leaf
salt and freshly ground black pepper

1. Place all the ingredients, except the reserved stick of celery, into a large saucepan, bring to the boil, reduce the heat, cover, and simmer for 25–30 minutes.

2. Strain through a sieve lined with 3–4 layers of wet cheesecloth. If the consommé is at all cloudy, clarify it (see above).

3. For the garnish, slice the reserved stick of celery into neat narrow slices and simmer in a little lightly salted boiling water for 5 minutes. Drain well.

4. Return the consommé to the pan, taste, and adjust the seasoning, if necessary, and heat through. To serve, spoon a few slices of the celery garnish into the bottom of each of 6 bowls and ladle the consommé in on top. Serve immediately.

Opposite: Celery Consommé and Mushroom Consommé (recipe overleaf).

Mushroom Consommé

Friends always joke that my motto is "if in doubt, splash in a bit of alcohol!". It's probably true. And it works here—this recipe really is improved by the subtle sweetness of the madeira or sherry.

Serves 6

1½ quarts chicken stock (see p.37)
⅓ cup madeira or medium sherry
1 onion, peeled and quartered
¾ lb button mushrooms, chopped
salt and freshly ground black pepper

1. Reserving a few mushrooms for garnish, put all the ingredients into a large saucepan, bring to the boil, reduce the heat, and simmer for 25–30 minutes.

2. Strain the consommé through a sieve lined with 3–4 layers of wet cheesecloth.

3. Clarify the consommé (see p.44). You will need double the quantities of the clarifying ingredients.

4. Ladle a little of the consommé into a small pan and bring to the boil. Slice the reserved mushrooms and drop them into the pan. Reduce the heat and cook gently for 4–5 minutes.

5. To serve, return the clear consommé to the heat, taste and adjust the seasoning, if necessary, and heat through. Ladle the consommé into 6 bowls. Spoon a few of the cooked mushroom slices into each.

Beef Tea

This traditional "tonic" soup also makes an excellent starter.

Serves 4–6

2lb top round of beef, cubed
1 quart water
1 onion, quartered
bouquet garni made with 3–4 sprigs fresh parsley,
    3–4 sprigs fresh thyme, 1 bay leaf
salt and freshly ground black pepper

1. Put the beef pieces into a food processor and process until well ground. Place in a large bowl or jug with all the other ingredients. Cover and leave to infuse for about 2 hours.

2. Stand the bowl or jug in a large pan of very gently simmering water and cook for at least 2 hours.

3. Strain the stock, adjust the seasoning, and serve.

Right: A Victorian advertisement for beef tea.

Clear Vegetable Soup with Pasta Cushions

This is an elegant and light starter and suits the addition of a few cushions of vegetarian ravioli or other pasta. Because we are all too busy to make our own pasta, I am not including a recipe to make the pasta cushions: just buy some ready-made ones and spoon them in at the last minute.

Serves 6

1¾ quarts vegetable stock (see p.41)
2 parsnips, peeled and chopped
4 carrots, scraped and chopped
2 sticks celery, chopped
2 onions, peeled and quartered
4 garlic cloves , peeled and roughly chopped
bouquet garni made with 4–5 sprigs fresh parsley,
    4 sprigs fresh thyme, 4 sprigs fresh marjoram
1 thick slice fennel
salt and freshly ground black pepper
12 cushions of vegetarian ravioli
sprigs of fresh parsley or chervil, to garnish

1. Put all the ingredients except the pasta into a large saucepan and bring to the boil. Reduce the heat and simmer for 45 minutes.

2. Strain the soup through a sieve lined with 3–4 layers of wet cheesecloth and return to the pan. Taste, and adjust the seasoning, if necessary. Bring the soup back to the boil.

3. Meanwhile, bring a separate pan of lightly salted water to the boil, drop in the pasta and simmer for 2–3 minutes, or as instructed on the packet.

4. To serve, ladle the soup into 6 bowls and spoon 2 cushions of pasta into each one. Float a small sprig of parsley or chervil top.

Vegetable Soup with Tiny Meatballs

If you prefer, use pork or chicken meat to make the little meatballs and make them a little bigger. The mixture of vegetables can also be changed to include radish, celery, fennel, snowpeas, cucumber, or zucchini.

Serves 6

For the meatballs:
1lb minced lamb
4oz ready-to-use dried apricots
2 garlic cloves, peeled
1 tablespoon chopped fresh cilantro
½ teaspoon ground cumin
salt and freshly ground black pepper

For the soup:
1¾ quarts chicken stock (see p.37)
    or lamb stock (see p.38)
bouquet garni made with 1 piece lemon zest,
    3–4 sprigs fresh marjoram and 2 garlic cloves
4 carrots, scraped and cut into fine julienne strips
6 scallions, cut into narrow julienne strips
2–3 turnips, peeled and cut into julienne strips
1 red pepper, cored, deseeded, and cut into narrow
    julienne strips
salt and freshly ground black pepper
sprigs of flat-leafed parsley or cilantro, to garnish

1. To make the meatballs, put all the ingredients into a food processor and blend together. Working with wet hands, shape the mixture into little balls approximately ½-inch in diameter. Set aside.

2. To make the soup, put the stock into a large saucepan with the bouquet garni and boil to reduce by about one third.

3. Carefully drop the meatballs into the gently simmering liquid. Allow to cook for 5 minutes, then add the strips of vegetable and cook for a further 3–4 minutes.

4. Taste the soup and adjust the seasoning, if necessary. Ladle the soup into 6 bowls, ensuring that each portion has a few meatballs and a good mixture of vegetable strips. Garnish with sprigs of parsley or cilantro.

Ginger Consommé with Lobster

If you prefer, use a good fish stock for this consommé and add a splash of dry white wine before boiling to reduce it.

Serves 6

1¾ quarts chicken stock (see p.37)
1 inch piece fresh root ginger, peeled and cut
    into tiny, narrow strips
1 lobster tail
6 scallions, cut diagonally into neat slices
6 sprigs fresh cilantro, to garnish

1. Put the stock and the ginger into a pan and boil to reduce by one third.

2. Cut the lobster tail in half lengthways and add to the stock. Simmer gently for 15–20 minutes. Lift out the lobster tail and remove the meat from the shell. Discard the shell and put the lobster meat back into the stock. Add the scallions and simmer for 2–3 minutes to allow the ingredients to heat through.

3. Taste the consommé and adjust the seasoning, if necessary. Ladle it into 6 bowls, ensuring that each portion has a few slices of scallion and a couple of pieces of lobster meat. Garnish with fresh cilantro or chervil.

Bamboo Shoot and Mushroom Soup

This Chinese-style clear broth has a hint of ginger to enhance the flavor of the shredded bamboo and mushrooms.

Serves 6

1¾ quarts chicken stock (see p.37) or
    vegetable stock (see p.41)
4oz canned bamboo shoots, drained and cut
    into thin strips
8oz button mushrooms, or drained canned
    straw mushrooms, thinly sliced
1 inch piece of fresh root ginger, peeled and
    cut into 4 pieces
2 tablespoons light soy sauce
2 teaspoons dry sherry
1 teaspoon wine vinegar
2 teaspoons cornstarch
salt and freshly ground black pepper
sprigs of fresh cilantro or chervil, to garnish

1. Put the stock, bamboo shoots, mushrooms, ginger, soy sauce, sherry, and vinegar into a large saucepan and bring slowly to the boil. Simmer for 10–15 minutes. Remove the pieces of ginger and discard.

2. Mix the cornstarch with a little cold water and stir into the soup. Allow the soup to simmer gently until slightly thickened.

3. Taste the soup and adjust the seasoning, if necessary. Ladle it into 6 bowls. To garnish, float a few small sprigs of cilantro or chervil on the surface of each.

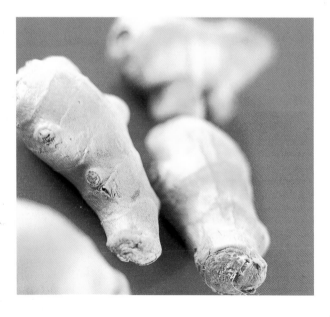

Left: Fresh root ginger.
Right: Bamboo Shoot and Mushroom Soup.

Miso Soup with White Radish and Tofu

Japanese miso-flavored soups are great with just a few *al dente* vegetables added—choose from spinach, Chinese cabbage, lotus roots, mushrooms, bamboo shoots, palm hearts, asparagus spears, strips of red pepper, slices of cucumber, or green beans. And, instead of tofu, you can use cubes of fresh chicken simmered in the stock with ginger and leeks.

Serves 6

1¾ quarts vegetable stock (see p.41)
    or chicken stock (see p.37)
4–6 tablespoons white or yellow miso, depending on
    how strong you wish the flavor to be
1 leek, trimmed, washed and very thinly sliced
1 teaspoon grated or very finely chopped
    fresh root ginger
12oz white radish (mooli)
12oz tofu, cut into ¾-inch cubes
2 teaspoons mirin (Japanese sweet rice wine) or
    medium sherry
toasted sesame seeds, to garnish

1. Put the stock, miso, leeks, and ginger into a saucepan and bring to the boil. Simmer for 5 minutes.

2. Peel the white radish and cut into slices ½-inch thick, then cut each slice into strips. Add to the stock, reduce the heat and simmer, partially covered, for 8–10 minutes, until the radish is beginning to soften.

3. Add the tofu and mirin and blend thoroughly.

4. Serve the soup sprinkled with toasted sesame seeds.

Opposite: Miso Soup with White Radish and Tofu.

THE CREAM OF THE CROP

Thick smooth soups are among the most comforting and luxurious of foods. They satisfy on chilly days in fall or winter, they nurture the body during illness, they make a soothing lunchtime treat, and they can feature on any dinner party menu as an indulgent first course.

Creamy soups are usually made by puréeing the cooked ingredients with the stock in which they were simmered. If the mixture contains potato, root vegetables, rice or ground rice, semolina, or other grains and pulses, the pulverizing process will generally give a smooth full-bodied soup. If the blend is too thick, stir in a little milk or stock.

If a creamy soup is too thin, it can be thickened in several ways:

- Use a mixture of flour and water or milk. Carefully blend a little flour with a little cold water or cold milk to give a smooth paste. Gradually mix in a spoonful or two of the stock or puréed soup, mix thoroughly, then stir into the soup. Allow the soup to boil for 2–3 minutes to cook the flour and thicken the mixture. Instead of wheat flour, use arrowroot, potato flour, cornstarch, rice flour, or kuzu (the Japanese equivalent of arrowroot); see p.26 for the amounts of these thickening agents to use in place of 1 tablespoon of wheat flour.
- Mashed potato: mix a couple of tablespoons of mashed potato with a little butter, cream, or milk and stir into the soup.
- Make a *beurre manié*: work 1 tablespoon flour into 1 tablespoon softened butter and add in small pieces to the soup; allow the soup to boil gently for 2–3 minutes to cook the flour and thicken the soup.
- Make a *crème maniée*: work flour into thick cream and use as for beurre manié.
- Mix egg yolk and cream, which gives a velvety silky texture to the soup: beat an egg yolk with 1–2 tablespoons heavy cream and strain into a small bowl. Mix in a little of the hot soup, remove the soup from the heat and carefully add the egg mixture. Allow the soup to heat through but do not let it boil as this will cause it to curdle.

Right: Prawn Bisque.

Shrimp Bisque

This makes a delicious summer appetizer or lunchtime main course.

Serves 4

6 tablespoons butter
2 shallots, peeled and finely chopped
1 carrot, scraped and chopped small
2 sticks celery, cut into small pieces
1½ quarts fish stock (see p.40)
¼–⅓ cup dry white wine
juice of ½ lemon
4 sprigs parsley
1 bay leaf
6 black peppercorns
12oz cooked shrimp in their shells
3 tablespoons all-purpose flour
1½ tablespoons tomato purée
2 tablespoons sweet sherry or brandy
salt and freshly ground black pepper
⅔ cup heavy cream
1 tablespoon finely chopped fresh tarragon
sprigs of fresh tarragon, to garnish

1. Melt 4 tablespoons of the butter in a pan, add the shallots, carrots, and celery, cover the pan, and sweat over a gentle heat for 4–5 minutes. Add the stock, wine, lemon juice, parsley, bay leaf, and peppercorns and bring to the boil. Cover the pan and simmer gently for 15–20 minutes.

2. Add the whole shrimp and simmer for 3–4 minutes. Lift out with a slotted spoon, cool, and remove their shells.

3. Set the shrimp aside. Add the shells to the stock, bring back to the boil, partially cover and simmer for 20 minutes. Strain through a fine sieve into a clean saucepan.

4. Put the shrimp in a food processor or blender with a little of the stock and process. Add to the stock.

5. Mix the flour with the remaining softened butter. Gradually blend with 2–3 tablespoons of the stock and add to the pan with the tomato purée and sherry or brandy. Taste and season. Bring to the boil.

6. Just before serving, stir in the cream and finely chopped tarragon, warming the soup again, but being careful not to let it boil. Serve the soup garnished with sprigs of fresh tarragon.

Chicken, Asparagus, and Lemon Soup

Soups made just from chicken can be a little bland, but combine the meat with fresh asparagus and lemon juice and you have a perfect summer soup.

Serves 6

2 tablespoons light olive oil
1 onion, peeled and roughly chopped
3 chicken breast halves, trimmed
    of fat and sinew and cut into pieces
1³/₄ quarts chicken stock (see p.37)
2 thinly pared strips of lemon rind
1 teaspoon fresh thyme leaves
1¹/₂ lb fresh asparagus spears, trimmed
juice of 1 lemon
handful of fresh basil leaves, torn into pieces
1 egg yolk
1¹/₄ cups light cream

1. Heat the oil in a large saucepan. Add the onion and fry very gently until transparent. Add the chicken to the pan and cook over a fairly high heat for 2–3 minutes, stirring all the time.

2. Add the chicken stock, lemon rind, and thyme to the pan and simmer for 10 minutes. Remove the lemon rind.

3. Meanwhile, blanch the asparagus tips in boiling water for 1–2 minutes. Drain, refresh in cold water, and drain again. Reserve a few of the smallest tips for garnish.

4. Add the asparagus tips and the basil leaves to the pan, cover and simmer for 30 minutes, or until the asparagus is well cooked.

5. Allow the mixture to cool, then process it in a blender or food processor until very smooth. Pour back into the pan.

6. Beat the egg yolk with a little of the cream, strain into a small bowl, add a little of the soup and mix thoroughly. Add to the soup with the lemon juice and the rest of the cream and allow to warm through gently, being careful not to let it boil.

7. Serve the soup garnished with a few of the reserved asparagus tips and a sprig of fresh basil.

Mushroom, Hazelnut, and Roasted Garlic Soup

Hazelnuts add an unusual and delicate flavor to this rich mix. This is excellent as a winter appetizer or lunchtime filler.

Serves 6

10 large garlic cloves, skins left on
2–3 tablespoons light olive oil
1¹/₂ lb mushrooms, sliced
¹/₄ cup ground hazelnuts
2¹/₄ cups vegetable stock (see p.41)
salt and freshly ground black pepper
¹/₂ teaspoon grated nutmeg
scant 2 cups milk
²/₃ cup heavy cream
sprigs of fresh tarragon, to garnish

1. Preheat the oven to 400°F/200°C. Brush the garlic cloves with a little olive oil and roast in the oven for 15–20 minutes. When cool enough to handle, squeeze the flesh from the skins, and mash.

2. Heat the oil in a large saucepan, add the mushrooms and cook gently over a low heat for 2–3 minutes, until the juices begin to run out. Put the lid on the pan and simmer gently for 5 minutes.

3. Stir the mashed garlic and the ground hazelnuts into the mixture, then add the stock, nutmeg, and salt and pepper. Stir the ingredients together. Cover the pan and simmer gently for 10–15 minutes.

4. Allow the mixture to cool, then purée it in a blender or food processor until really smooth. Return to the pan and stir in the milk. Taste and adjust the seasoning, if necessary. Allow the mixture to heat through, without boiling. Just before serving, stir in the cream. Serve the soup garnished with fresh tarragon.

Left: Chicken, Asparagus, and Lemon Soup.

Cheesy Potato and Leek Soup

This deliciously creamy vegetable soup has the added bite of tangy mature Cheddar cheese.

Serves 4–6

2–3 tablespoons light olive oil
1 onion, peeled and roughly chopped
2 garlic cloves, peeled and chopped
1lb leeks, cut into 1 inch pieces
1lb potatoes, peeled and roughly chopped
1½ quarts chicken stock (see p.37)
   or vegetable stock (see p.41)
1 teaspoon fresh thyme or marjoram leaves
salt and freshly ground black pepper
1 egg yolk
⅔ cup heavy cream
1 cup mature Cheddar cheese, grated

1. Heat the oil in a large saucepan. Add the onions and fry gently until transparent. Add the garlic and cook gently for 2 minutes. Add the leeks and potatoes, cover the pan, and sweat over a low heat for 10 minutes, until the vegetables are softened but not browned.

2. Add the stock, thyme or marjoram, and salt and pepper. Bring to the boil, reduce the heat, cover the pan, and simmer for 30 minutes, or until all the vegetables are soft.

3. Allow the mixture to cool, then purée it in a food processor or blender until really smooth. Pour back into the pan.

4. Blend together the egg yolk and cream and stir into the soup. Heat through gently, being careful not to allow it to boil or it will curdle. Just before serving, stir in the grated cheddar.

Pumpkin and Sweet Potato Soup

Use pear-shaped butternut squash or pumpkin to make a thick warming autumn or winter soup. Pumpkin needs plenty of seasoning so add more spices and herbs to suit.

Serves 6–8

2–3 tablespoons light olive oil
2 onions, peeled and roughly chopped
1 leek, cut into 1 inch pieces
2 garlic cloves, peeled and chopped
1½ lb pumpkin, deseeded, peeled, and cut
   into chunks
8oz sweet potato, peeled and cut into chunks
1¾ quarts chicken stock (see p.37) or
   vegetable stock (see p.41)
1¾ cups coconut cream
1 bay leaf
1 teaspoon fresh thyme leaves
1 teaspoon grated nutmeg
large pinch medium curry powder
large pinch ground allspice
salt and freshly ground black pepper
⅔ cup heavy cream
⅔ – 1 cup parmesan cheese, grated
fresh chives, to garnish

1. Heat the oil in a large saucepan. Add the onion and leek and gently fry until transparent. Add the garlic and cook gently for 2 minutes. Add the pumpkin, sweet potato, stock, coconut cream, bay leaf, thyme, nutmeg, curry powder, allspice, and salt and pepper and bring to the boil. Cover the pan, reduce the heat, and simmer gently for 30 minutes, or until the vegetables are really soft.

2. Allow the mixture to cool, then purée it in a blender or food processor. Return to the pan and reheat. If the soup seems too thick, stir in a little milk. Just before serving, stir in the parmesan cheese.

3. To serve, pour the soup into bowls and garnish with snipped fresh chives.

Right: Pumpkin and Sweet Potato Soup.

Zucchini, Sherry, and Fava Bean Soup

The fava beans give body to the thinner texture of the zucchini, while the sherry adds a subtle depth to the flavor.

Serves 6

2–3 tablespoons light olive oil
2 large onions, peeled and roughly chopped
2–3 teaspoons sugar
1lb zucchini, sliced
1lb shelled fava beans, thawed if frozen
1 ½ quarts chicken stock (see p.37), ham stock
    (see p.38), or vegetable stock (see p.41)
1–2 tablespoons dry sherry
2 teaspoons fresh thyme leaves
1 tablespoon chopped fresh marjoram
salt and freshly ground black pepper
1 egg yolk
²⁄₃ cup heavy cream
crispy croûtons, to garnish (see p.123)

1. Heat the oil in a large saucepan. Add the onions and fry gently until soft and translucent. Add the sugar and continue to cook for 3–4 minutes.

2. Add the zucchini, fava beans, stock, sherry, thyme, marjoram, and salt and pepper. Bring to the boil, reduce the heat, cover the pan, and simmer gently for 35–40 minutes.

3. Allow the mixture to cool a little. Purée it in a food processor or blender until really smooth. Then pass through a sieve to remove all the coarse skins from the fava beans. Return to the pan.

4. Blend the egg yolk with a little of the cream and strain into the soup. Return the pan to the stove and heat through gently until smooth. Stir in the remaining cream and serve garnished with the croûtons.

Cream of Stilton and Broccoli Soup

Blue cheeses blend beautifully with broccoli, turning an everyday vegetable into a rich thick soup that is packed with nutrition and flavor.

Serves 4–6

2–3 tablespoons light olive oil
2 onions, peeled and chopped
2lb broccoli, stalks removed
    and stems and florets cut into chunks
1 quart chicken stock (see p.37)
    or vegetable stock (see p.41)
½ teaspoon grated nutmeg
8oz Stilton (or other strongly
    flavored blue cheese), crumbled
salt and freshly ground black pepper
⅓ cup Greek yoghurt
⅓ cup light cream
toasted almonds, to garnish

1. Heat the oil in a large saucepan. Add the onion and gently fry until transparent. Add the broccoli, stock and nutmeg. Bring to the boil, reduce the heat, cover the pan and simmer for 15–20 minutes, until the broccoli is really soft.

2. Allow the mixture to cool, purée in a food processor or blender, then return to the pan. Add the Stilton cheese, taste, and adjust the seasoning if necessary, and reheat the soup.

3. Just before serving, add the yoghurt and cream, warming the soup through but being careful not to allow it to boil. Serve garnished with a few toasted almonds.

Left: Zucchini, Sherry, and Fava Bean Soup.

Red Pepper and Tomato Soup

This is one of my favorite soups—absolutely full of flavor, including the aromatic tang of fresh lime.

Serves 4–6

2–3 tablespoons light olive oil
3 large red sweet peppers, cored, deseeded,
    and roughly sliced
2 onions, peeled and chopped
2 garlic cloves, peeled and sliced
6 tomatoes, skinned and chopped
1 tablespoon tomato purée
2 teaspoons fresh or 1 teaspoon dried thyme leaves
¼ cup all-purpose flour
1 quart vegetable stock (see p.41) or
    chicken stock (see p.37)
salt and freshly ground black pepper
the juice of 1 lime
a handful of shredded fresh basil leaves
fresh basil, to garnish

1. Heat the oil in a large saucepan. Add the peppers and onions. Cover the pan and sweat the vegetables over a gentle heat for 15–20 minutes so that they soften but do not brown.

2. Add the garlic and cook for 2 minutes. Add the tomatoes, tomato purée, thyme, and flour to the pan, stir well and cook for 2 minutes, stirring all the time.

3. Remove the pan from the heat and gradually add the stock. Return to the heat and bring to the boil, stirring all the time. Season with salt and pepper, reduce the heat, cover the pan and simmer for 15–20 minutes.

4. Allow the mixture to cool, then purée it in a food processor or blender until really smooth. Pour back into the pan to heat. Just before serving, stir in the lime juice and shredded basil leaves. Serve garnished with more shredded or whole basil leaves.

Tomato, Eggplant, and Crab Soup

Roasting the vegetables for this soup before adding them brings out all their sweetness and subtle flavors. The soup is great served hot or chilled.

Serves 4–6

4 eggplant
2lb ripe tomatoes, halved
6 garlic cloves, skins left on
4–5 tablespoons light olive oil
2 onions, peeled and roughly chopped
1½ quarts chicken stock (see p.37)
    or vegetable stock (see p.41)
2 tablespoons chopped fresh tarragon
1 tablespoon tomato purée
⅔ cup dry white wine
12oz canned crab meat, drained
    and broken into flakes
salt and freshly ground black pepper
sprigs of tarragon, to garnish

1. Preheat the oven to 400°F/200°C. Peel the eggplant thinly and cut the flesh into cubes about 1-inch square. Put into a baking tray and drizzle over a little olive oil. Put the tomato halves and the garlic cloves on a separate baking tray and brush with a little olive oil.

2. Roast the vegetables and garlic for 30 minutes. After 15–20 minutes, check the garlic. If it has begun to dry and turn brown, remove it. Cool and then squeeze the garlic pulp from the skins. Scoop the tomato flesh and juice from the tomato skins, discarding the skins.

3. Heat the remaining olive oil in a large saucepan and gently fry the onions until soft and transparent. Add the eggplant, tomato, garlic, stock, tarragon, white wine, and tomato purée. Bring to the boil, reduce the heat, cover the pan, and simmer for 30 minutes.

4. Allow the mixture to cool, then purée it in a food processor or blender until smooth. Return to the pan and stir in the crab meat. Taste and adjust the seasoning, if necessary, and heat the soup through. Serve garnished with sprigs of fresh tarragon.

Right: Tomato, Eggplant, and Crab Soup.

Chestnut and Bacon Soup

If you can't find fresh chestnuts, buy the cooked, peeled, and vacuum-packed ones that are available in supermarkets. This is a sweet, creamy, and really delicious autumn or winter soup.

Serves 6–8

1lb chestnuts, shelled weight
2–3 tablespoons light olive oil
2 onions, peeled and roughly chopped
4 slices bacon, cut into small pieces
3 carrots, scraped and roughly chopped
2 sticks celery, roughly chopped
1¾ quarts chicken stock (see p.37) or
    ham stock (see p.38)
2 tablespoons chopped fresh parsley
2 teaspoons fresh or 1 teaspoon dried thyme
2 bay leaves
salt and freshly ground black pepper
small pieces crispy bacon, to garnish

1. If using fresh whole chestnuts, put them into a large pan of cold water, bring to the boil and boil for 4–5 minutes. Drain, cool, and peel off the outer and inner skins. (If using ready skinned chestnuts leave out this first stage.)

2. Heat the oil in a large saucepan. Add the onion and bacon and gently fry until the onion is transparent but not browned. Add the carrots and celery, cover the pan, and cook gently for 2–3 minutes.

3. Add the chestnuts, stock, and herbs, bring to the boil, reduce the heat, cover the pan, and simmer gently for 1 hour, or until the chestnuts are really soft and beginning to fall apart. Discard the bay leaves.

4. Allow the mixture to cool, then purée it in a food processor or blender until smooth. If it seems too thick, stir in a little milk. Taste and adjust the seasoning, if necessary. Serve garnished with crispy bacon.

Curried Parsnip and Carrot Soup

This is a winner. The color, texture, and flavor seems to be a favorite with almost everyone who tries it.

Serves 4–6

2–3 tablespoons light olive oil
2 onions, peeled and roughly chopped
2–3 teaspoons medium curry powder
½ teaspoon ground cilantro
½ teaspoon ground cumin
2lb parsnips, peeled and sliced
2lb carrots, scraped and sliced
1¾ quarts chicken stock (see p.37)
    or vegetable stock (see p.41)
salt and freshly ground black pepper
⅔ cup heavy cream
toasted pine nuts, to garnish

1. Heat the oil in a large saucepan. Add the onion and gently fry until transparent. Add the curry powder, cilantro, and cumin, mix well and cook for 1–2 minutes.

2. Add the parsnips and carrots, cover the pan, and sweat over a gentle heat. Add the stock. Bring the pan to the boil, reduce the heat, cover, and simmer gently for 25–30 minutes.

3. Allow the mixture to cool, then purée it in a food processor or blender until smooth. Return the mixture to the pan and warm through.

4. Just before serving, add the cream and taste and adjust the seasoning, if necessary. Warm through again, being careful not to allow the soup to boil. Serve garnished with toasted pine nuts.

Left: Chestnut and Bacon Soup.

Beet, Ham, and Dill Soup

The rich sweetness of beets is wonderful mixed with the ham and dill. The color of this soup is stunning— serve it in white bowls for a really dramatic effect.

Serves 4–6

2–3 tablespoons light olive oil
2 onions, peeled and roughly chopped
2 teaspoons caster sugar
2 garlic cloves, peeled and chopped
1lb cooked beets, peeled and chopped
    into small chunks
4oz button mushrooms
2 dessert apples, peeled, cored and chopped
¾ lb ham, cut into small cubes
1½ quarts ham stock (see p.38)
    or chicken stock (see p.37)
2–3 teaspoons chopped fresh dill, chopped
salt and freshly ground black pepper
juice of 1 lemon
⅔ cup heavy cream

For the garnish:
sprigs of fresh dill
small dice of cooked beets

1. Heat the oil in a large saucepan. Add the onions and garlic and gently fry until transparent. Add the sugar and continue cooking until the onions are golden brown.

2. Add the beets, mushrooms, apples, ham, stock, dill, and salt and pepper. Bring the mixture to the boil, reduce the heat, cover the pan, and simmer gently for 25–30 minutes.

3. Allow the mixture to cool then purée it in a food processor or blender until smooth. Return to the pan, add the lemon juice, and taste, adjusting the seasoning, if necessary. Reheat gently.

4. Just before serving, stir in the cream and allow the soup to heat through again. Serve garnished with a spoonful of tiny beet cubes and a sprig of dill.

Right: Beet, Ham, and Dill Soup.

MAKING
A MEAL
OF IT

Fashionable soup bars are beginning to change the way we eat at lunchtime. They offer unusual combinations that satisfy midday hunger but also offer a really healthy alternative to all those other fast foods that we grab during the precious half hour or so that we allow ourselves these days.

O f course, sandwiches are fine and fruit and vegetable juices and smoothies are great. But sometimes, don't you just crave something hot and tasty and really easy to eat? Something that really activates the taste buds, that sends off curling trails of steam and wonderful smells. A big mug or bowl of soup is the answer—full of the crunchy texture of mixed vegetables, juicy pieces of meat, succulent chunks of lobster or crab, the nourishment of beans, pulses, nuts and grains, handfuls of fresh herbs, and all the color and exciting flavor of fresh ingredients. Just about any combination is possible in the creation of exciting, filling mixtures that really do offer a meal in a bowl.

As Isabella Beeton wrote in 1861,

The principal art in composing good rich soup is so to proportion the several ingredients that the flavor of one shall not predominate over another, and that all the articles of which it is composed, shall form an agreeable whole. To accomplish this, care must be taken that the roots and herbs are perfectly well cleaned, and that the water is proportioned to the quantity of meat and other ingredients.

The principals remain the same today and the most successful of modern soup bars and kitchens are including wonderfully balanced blends of interesting and tasty ingredients. Soup Opera, London's first gourmet soup bar, has created Thai Green Vegetable Curry, Chicken Pot Pie, Caribbean Chicken, Sugar Snap Pea with Avocado and Mint, and Lobster in Mango and Ginger Coulis. Summer soups have included Shitake Tuna, Grilled Chicken, Walnuts and Grapes, Summer Rice with Pimentos, and Red Gazpacho. As they said in press releases, "Promising to dispel any pre-conceived ideas about soup, Soup Opera's enticing menu puts soup firmly back on the table as a healthy, restorative meal to suit all tastes and appetites."

Moroccan Lamb and Chickpea Soup

This is a spicy mixture of all the delicious meat and vegetables normally served on a bed of couscous.

Serves 6

2–3 tablespoons olive oil
2 onions, peeled, halved and very thinly sliced
2 garlic cloves, peeled finely chopped
1 teaspoon ground ginger
1 teaspoon ground cumin
1 teaspoon paprika
1lb lamb steaks, cut off the bone, trimmed of any fat and cut into strips or chunks
salt and freshly ground black pepper
1 x 14oz can chopped tomatoes
1½ quarts chicken stock (see p.37) or lamb stock (see p.38)
3 carrots, scraped and thinly sliced
2 zucchini, thinly sliced
2 x 14oz cans chickpeas, drained and rinsed
2 tablespoons chopped fresh cilantro
2 tablespoons chopped fresh parsley
fresh cilantro or flat-leafed parsley, to garnish

1. Heat the oil in a large saucepan. Add the onions and gently fry until soft and translucent. Add the garlic and fry gently for 2 minutes.

2. Add the ginger, cumin, and paprika to the pan and cook for 1 minute. Add the lamb and fry over a high heat until the meat is sealed on all sides. Add the tomatoes, stock, and a little salt and pepper, bring to the boil, reduce the heat, cover, and simmer gently for 10 minutes.

3. Add the carrots and cook for a further 15–20 minutes. Add the zucchini and cook for 5 minutes. Add the chickpeas, cilantro, and parsley and continue cooking until the chickpeas are heated through.

4. Before serving, taste and adjust the seasoning, if necessary. Serve the soup garnished with sprigs of fresh cilantro or flat-leafed parsley.

Opposite: Moroccan Lamb and Chickpea Soup.

Duck Soup with Ginger and Chinese Cabbage

This is an easy oriental-style soup with the subtle flavors of root ginger and lemon grass.

Serves 6

3 tablespoons olive oil
4 duck breasts
salt and freshly ground black pepper
1 inch piece of fresh root ginger, peeled and cut into narrow strips
1/2 tablespoon sesame oil
6 scallions, trimmed and sliced diagonally
1 3/4 quarts chicken stock (see p.37)
1 tablespoon dry sherry
1 tablespoon chopped lemon grass
3 teaspoons arrowroot or cornstarch
3/4 lb Chinese cabbage, finely shredded
toasted sesame seeds, to garnish

1. Heat 2 tablespoons of the olive oil in a frying pan. Season the duck breasts with salt and pepper, put in the pan and fry, skin side down, for 5 minutes until browned. Turn over and fry the other side for 5 minutes. Remove from the pan and drain on kitchen paper. Cut the duck meat into neat pieces.

2. Blanch the strips of ginger in a little boiling water for 30 seconds, then drain and pat dry.

3. Heat the remaining olive oil and the sesame oil in a large saucepan. Add the scallions and gently fry them for 2–3 minutes. Add the ginger, duck meat, stock, sherry, and lemon grass and bring slowly to the boil. Cover the pan and simmer gently for 15–20 minutes.

4. Mix the arrowroot or cornstarch with a little cold water and add to the pan. Stir and cook for 1–2 minutes, until the mixture has thickened slightly. Add the shredded Chinese cabbage and cook for a further 3–4 minutes, until the cabbage leaves have wilted. Taste and adjust the seasoning, if necessary.

5. Serve the soup garnished with a sprinkling of toasted sesame seeds.

Opposite: Duck Soup with Ginger and Chinese Cabbage.
Overleaf: Double Bean and Pork Hot Pot.

Double Bean and Pork Hot Pot

Green beans, navy beans, and pork combine to make a satisfying soup that is almost a rich stew.

Serves 6–8

1 1/4 cups navy navy beans
2–3 tablespoons olive oil
2 large onions, peeled, halved, and thinly sliced
2 garlic cloves, peeled and finely chopped
1 teaspoons paprika
2 sticks celery, neatly sliced
1 lb pork shoulder, trimmed of any fat, and cut into neat cubes
1 3/4 quarts chicken stock (see p.37)
1x 14oz can chopped tomatoes
2 tablespoons chopped fresh parsley
1 tablespoon chopped fresh marjoram
leaves from 3–4 sprigs fresh thyme
1 bay leaf
3/4 lb green beans, or flat (stringless) green beans, cut into 1 inch pieces
2 tablespoons all-purpose flour
1/4 cup softened butter
salt and freshly ground black pepper
sprigs of flat-leafed parsley, to garnish

1. Soak the navy beans overnight in cold water. Rinse and drain. Put into a large saucepan, cover with water, bring to the boil, and skim off any scum that rises. Rinse in cold water and drain.

2. Heat the oil in a large saucepan. Add the onions and garlic and gently fry them until translucent. Add the paprika and celery and stir over the heat for 2 minutes.

3. Add the pork and brown. Add the stock, tomatoes, navy beans and herbs. Cover the pan and simmer for 1 1/2 hours, or until the pork and beans are tender.

4. Add the green beans to the pan and cook for a further 7–8 minutes, until just soft.

5. Remove the bay leaf. Taste and adjust the seasoning, if necessary. Mix the flour and butter together and add in small pieces. Boil for 2–3 minutes, then serve garnished with sprigs of parsley.

Green Vegetable and Lentil Soup

This is an excellent vitamin-packed lunch, full of wonderful flavor. Using vegetable stock instead of chicken stock makes it suitable for vegetarians.

Serves 6–8

2–3 tablespoons light olive oil
2 bunches scallions, thinly sliced
2 garlic cloves, peeled and thinly sliced
½ cup brown lentils
2 sticks celery, thinly sliced
2¼ quarts chicken stock (see p.37)
    or vegetable stock (see p.41)
4 tablespoons finely chopped fresh parsley
2 teaspoons fresh thyme leaves
salt and freshly ground black pepper
2 zucchini, cut into ½-inch cubes
2 x 14oz cans artichokes,
    drained and quartered
4oz snow peas or sugar snap peas,
    cut diagonally into ½-inch pieces
3 cups fresh spinach, thoroughly washed
2 tablespoons pesto

1. Heat the oil in a large saucepan. Add the scallions and garlic and gently fry them for 1–2 minutes.

2. Add the lentils, celery, stock, parsley, thyme, and a little salt and pepper. Cover the pan and simmer gently for 25–30 minutes, until the lentils are almost cooked.

3. Add the zucchini, artichokes, and snow peas or sugar snap peas to the pan and simmer for a further 8–10 minutes. Add the spinach and cook for 2 minutes. Stir in the pesto and taste, adjusting the seasoning, if necessary. Serve the soup at once.

Ham and Leek Soup

Allowing the leeks to sauté very slowly before adding the stock and other ingredients helps this soup develop a rich, sweet flavor.

Serves 6

2–3 tablespoons olive oil
1 onion, peeled amd finely chopped
4 garlic cloves, peeled and finely chopped
1lb leeks, very thinly sliced
2 carrots, scraped and cut into neat 1 inch julienne
    strips
¾ lb cooked ham, trimmed of any fat and cut
    into ½-inch cubes or into narrow strips
1¾ quarts chicken stock (see p.37), ham
    stock (see p.38), or vegetable stock (see p.41)
1 teaspoon dried or 1 tablespoon
    finely chopped fresh sage leaves
salt and freshly ground black pepper
beurre manié made with 2 teaspoons all-purpose flour
    and ¼ cup softened butter (see p.54)
⅔ cup heavy cream
chopped fresh parsley or sprigs of
    fresh thyme, to garnish

1. Heat the oil in a large saucepan. Add the onion and gently fry until soft and translucent. Add the garlic and fry gently for 2 minutes.

2. Add the leeks and carrots and sweat over a very low heat for 8–10 minutes without browning. Add the ham, stock, sage, and a little salt and pepper. Bring to the boil, reduce the heat, cover the pan, and simmer gently for 20–25 minutes.

3. Add the *beurre manié* in small pieces, stirring them into the soup, and simmer gently until slightly thickened. Stir in the cream and adjust the seasoning, if necessary.

4. Serve the soup garnished with chopped fresh parsley or sprigs of thyme.

Previous page: Green Vegetable and Lentil Soup.

Opposite: Ham and Leek Soup.

Red Cabbage, Beet, and Cumberland Sausage

The sweetness of the beets is wonderful in this fall or winter soup. The color is stunning and looks great served in white or green bowls.

Serves 6

1½ lb Cumberland, or other full-flavored, herbed sausages
2–3 tablespoons olive oil
2 onions, peeled, halved and thinly sliced
1 lb cooked beets, peeled and cut into 1-inch julienne strips
3 cups very finely shredded red cabbage
3 sweet dessert apples, peeled, cored and thinly sliced
2¼ quarts beef stock (see p.37)
1 tablespoon wine vinegar
2 teaspoons chopped fresh marjoram, chopped
2 teaspoons fresh thyme
1 tablespoon whole-grain mustard
1 teaspoon caraway seeds
salt and freshly ground black pepper
⅔ cup light cream
snipped chives or sprigs of fresh dill, to garnish

1. Preheat the oven to 350°F/180°C. Put the sausages in a roasting pan, cover with foil and bake for 45 minutes. Lift out of the pan, drain on kitchen paper, and cut into ½-inch slices or cubes.

2. Heat the oil in a large saucepan. Add the onions and gently fry them until soft and translucent. Add the beets, cabbage, apples, stock, wine vinegar, a little salt and pepper, marjoram, thyme, mustard, and caraway seeds, and a little seasoning. Bring to the boil, reduce the heat, cover the pan, and simmer for 45 minutes, or until the vegetables are almost tender.

3. Add the sausages to the pan and simmer for 10 minutes.

4. Just before serving the soup, stir in the cream and taste and adjust the seasoning, if necessary. Serve garnished with chives or dill.

Seafood and Sweet Potato Chowder

Use any kind of white fish for this, such as cod, haddock, or hake. Sweet potatoes go really well with fish and make an interesting change from other vegetables in this soup.

Serves 4–6

2–3 tablespoons light olive oil
2 onions, peeled and thinly sliced
2 garlic cloves, peeled and finely chopped
2 sticks celery, thinly sliced
1½ lb sweet potato (weighed after peeling), cut into ½-inch cubes
2¼ cups milk
3½ cups fish stock (see p.40)
¼ cup dry white wine
finely grated zest of ½ lemon
salt and freshly ground black pepper
1½ lb white fish fillets, boned and skinned
6 oz small shrimp
2 tablespoons finely chopped fresh parsley
⅔ cup heavy cream

1. Heat the oil in a large saucepan. Add the onion and gently fry until soft and translucent. Add the garlic and gently fry for 2 minutes.

2. Add the celery, sweet potato, milk, fish stock, wine, lemon zest, and a little salt and pepper, bring to the boil, reduce the heat, cover the pan, and simmer for 5 minutes, until the vegetables are beginning to soften.

3. Add the fish and simmer gently for a further 5 minutes.

4. Reserve a few shrimp to garnish the soup and stir the rest into the pan. Allow to heat through. Just before serving, taste and adjust the seasoning, if necessary. Stir in the cream and chopped parsley.

5. Serve the soup garnished with 2 or 3 of the reserved shrimp.

Opposite: Red Cabbage, Beet, and Cumberland Sausage Soup.

Overleaf: Seafood and Sweet Potato Chowder.

Pumpkin, Coconut, and Crunchy Vegetable Soup

This nourishing soup combines the sweetness of coconut milk with crisp vegetables and a hint of green chili.

Serves 6

2–3 tablespoons olive oil
2 onions, peeled and finely chopped
3 garlic cloves, peeled and finely chopped
1 small fresh green chili, chopped
1 teaspoon finely chopped or grated fresh root ginger
2 teaspoons chopped lemon grass, chopped
1 teaspoon ground turmeric
2 medium carrots, scraped and cut into
    1-inch julienne strips
2 sticks celery, sliced
4 small turnips, peeled and cut into ½-inch cubes
1lb pumpkin or butternut squash flesh,
    cut into ½ inch cubes
1½ quarts vegetable stock (see p.41)
8oz fresh green beans, cut into 1-inch pieces
1½ cups baby mushrooms, thinly sliced
1¾ cups coconut cream
2 tablespoons chopped fresh cilantro
2 tablespoons all-purpose flour
¼ cup softened butter
salt and freshly ground black pepper
1 cup fresh beansprouts
sprigs of flat-leafed parsley or cilantro, to garnish

1. Heat the oil in a large saucepan. Add the onion and garlic and gently fry until soft and translucent.

2. Add the chili, ginger, lemon grass, and turmeric and cook for 2 minutes. Add the carrots, celery, turnips, pumpkin, and stock and bring to the boil. Reduce the heat, cover the pan, and simmer gently for 5 minutes.

3. Add the green beans and cook for a further 8–10 minutes. Stir in the mushrooms, coconut cream, and cilantro and cook for 2–3 minutes.

4. Blend the flour and butter and add to the soup in small pieces. Simmer for 2–3 minutes, until slightly thickened.

5. Season. Just before serving, stir in the beansprouts. Serve immediately, garnished with parsley or cilantro.

Mushroom, Barley, and Red Pepper Soup

Barley adds a good old-fashioned heartiness to this soup—a real winter filler. Add more or different herbs to suit your own taste.

Serves 6

1 cup pearl barley
2–3 tablespoons olive oil
3 onions, peeled and finely chopped
2 garlic cloves, peeled and finely chopped
3 red peppers, cored, deseeded, and
    cut into 1-inch strips
¾ lb button mushrooms,
    halved and thinly sliced
1¾ quarts chicken stock (see p.37)
    or vegetable stock (see p.41)
2 tablespoons finely chopped fresh parsley
2 tablespoons fresh thyme leaves
2 bay leaves
1 tablespoon chopped fresh marjoram
2 strips lemon zest
salt and freshly ground black pepper
juice of 1 lemon
fresh thyme or marjoram, to garnish

1. Put the barley into a pan with plenty of cold water, bring to the boil, simmer for 2 minutes then drain. Return to the pan with plenty of fresh cold water and add a little salt. Bring to the boil, reduce the heat, partially cover, and simmer for 1 hour. Drain well.

2. Heat the oil in a large saucepan. Add the onion and garlic and gently fry until soft and translucent. Add the peppers and mushrooms and sweat over a gentle heat for 5 minutes.

3. Add the stock, cooked barley, herbs, lemon zest, and salt and pepper. Bring to the boil, reduce the heat, cover, and simmer for 45 minutes.

4. Remove the lemon zest and bay leaves and discard. Taste and adjust the seasoning, if necessary, and stir in the lemon juice. Serve the soup garnished with thyme or marjoram.

Previous page: Pumpkin, Coconut, and Crunchy Vegetable Soup.
Right: Mushroom, Barley, and Red Pepper Soup.

Chicken and Green Lentil Soup

The wholesome texture of puy lentils adds substance to a nourishing mix of tender chicken and fresh vegetables.

Serves 6–8

1¼ cups puy lentils
2–3 tablespoons olive oil
2 onions, peeled and very thinly sliced
6–8 garlic cloves, peeled and thinly sliced
2 carrots, scraped and cut into ½-inch cubes
4 small turnips, peeled and cut into small cubes
3 sticks celery, thinly sliced
4 chicken breast halves, trimmed of fat and sinew
2 tablespoons tomato purée
1 tablespoon fresh thyme leaves
2¼ quarts chicken stock (see p.37)
2 zucchini, cut into ½-inch cubes
⅔ cup light cream
2–3 tablespoons chopped fresh parsley
1¼ cups parmesan cheese, grated, to garnish

1. Put the puy lentils into a pan, cover with cold water, bring to the boil, reduce the heat, and simmer for 10 minutes. Drain.

2. Heat the oil in a large saucepan. Add the onions and garlic and gently fry them for 4–5 minutes until soft and translucent. Add the garlic and gently fry for 2–3 minutes. Add the carrots, turnips, and celery. Cover the pan and sweat the vegetables for 4–5 minutes.

3. Cut the chicken pieces into ¾-inch cubes. Put them in the pan and cook over a fairly high heat, turning until they are sealed all over.

4. Add the lentils, tomato purée, thyme leaves, and stock to the pan. Bring to the boil, reduce the heat, cover the pan, and simmer for 45–50 minutes, or until the lentils are tender.

5. Add the zucchini and simmer for a further 4–5 minutes, until the zucchini have just begun to soften.

6. Just before serving the soup, stir in the cream and chopped parsley and taste and adjust the seasoning, if necessary. Serve the soup with a little grated parmesan sprinkled over.

Opposite: Shrimp and Palm Heart Soup with Rice.

Shrimp and Palm Heart Soup with Rice

This unusual mixture is based on a Brazilian casserole from Rio which is normally served on a bed of white rice.

Serves 6–8

For the stock:
3 lb fresh small shrimp in their shells
1 onion, quartered
2 garlic cloves, roughly chopped
1 carrot, roughly chopped
3–4 sprigs fresh parsley
1 bay leaf
black peppercorns
2¼ quarts cold water

For the soup:
⅔ cupwhite long-grain rice
1–2 tablespoons olive oil
2 onions, finely chopped
1 green pepper, cut into ½-inch pieces
2 x 14oz cans chopped tomatoes
2–3 tablespoons chopped fresh parsley
salt and freshly ground black pepper
8 scallions, trimmed and
   cut diagonally into thin slices
2 x 14oz cans palm hearts,
   drained and sliced into ½-inch pieces

1. Peel the shrimp and put the shells and trimmings into a large pan with the onion, garlic, carrot, parsley, bay leaf, peppercorns, and water. Bring to the boil, skim off any scum, cover, and simmer for 35–40 minutes.

2. Strain the stock and pour it back into the pan. Add the rice and bring to the boil. Cover the pan and simmer very gently for 10–12 minutes.

3. In a separate saucepan, heat the oil and gently fry the onion and green pepper for 10–15 minutes, until soft. Add to the stock with the tomatoes, parsley and salt and pepper. Bring back to the boil and simmer for 5 minutes.

4. Blanch the scallions in boiling water for 2 minutes, then drain. Add the shrimp and palm hearts to the soup, heat through and serve garnished with the scallion slices.

Salmon, Fennel, and Cucumber Soup

This is like a juicy fish stew. The combination of fennel and salmon is deliciously subtle.

Serves 4- 6

1–2 tablespoons light olive oil
12 scallions, trimmed and cut
    diagonally into thin slices
1 head fennel, coarsely chopped
1 teaspoon chopped lemon grass
1 quart fish stock (see p.40)
2–3 tablespoons white wine
2 fresh salmon steaks, each
    approximately 4oz, skinned and boned
½ cucumber, cut into 1-inch julienne strips
    or into small cubes
2 tablespoons finely chopped fresh dill
crème maniée made with 2 tablespoons all-purpose
    flour blended with 2 tablespoons cream (see p.54)
salt and freshly ground black pepper
1 tablespoon lemon juice
sprigs of fresh dill, to garnish

1. Heat the oil in a large saucepan. Add the scallions and gently fry for 2 minutes. Add the fennel and lemon grass and sweat over a very gentle heat for 15 minutes, until softened but not browned.

2. Add the fish stock, white wine, and salmon steaks, cover the pan and simmer very gently for 10 minutes. Add the cucumber and dill and cook for a further 5 minutes.

3. Lift the salmon steaks out of the pan and flake them with a fork, removing any bones you may find. Return the fish flakes to the pan.

4. Stir small pieces of the *crème maniée* into the soup until it has slightly thickened. Add the lemon juice, and taste and adjust the seasoning, if necessary. Serve the soup garnished with sprigs of fresh dill.

Mexican Beef and Bean Soup

This soup contains all the ingredients of a beef chili.

Serves 6–8

⅔ cup dried kidney beans
⅔ cup dried Mexican black beans
2–3 tablespoons olive oil
2 onions, peeled and finely chopped
2 garlic cloves, peeled and finely chopped
1 medium red pepper, cored, deseeded, and diced
1 green pepper, cored, deseeded, and diced
½–1 jalapeno or other green chili
3 teaspoons ground cumin
2 teaspoons ground cilantro
2lb lean stewing beef, trimmed of
    any fat and cut into ¾-inch cubes
2 x 14oz cans chopped tomatoes
1¾ cup quarts beef stock (see p.37)
2 tablespoons tomato purée
salt and freshly ground black pepper

For the garnish:
2 tablespoons grated Cheddar cheese
12–16 small tortilla chips

1. Soak the kidney beans and black beans in separate bowls of cold water overnight. Drain and put into 2 large saucepans with enough cold water to well cover. Bring to the boil, reduce the heat and simmer for 20 minutes. Drain, rinse and drain again.

2. Heat the oil in a large saucepan. Add the onion and gently fry it until soft and translucent. Add the garlic and fry gently for 2 minutes. Add the diced red and green peppers and the chili. Cover the pan and sweat the vegetables for 5 minutes. Add the cumin and cilantro and fry for 1–2 minutes. Add the beef to the pan and stir over a fairly high heat to brown the meat all over.

3. Add the cooked beans, tomatoes, stock, tomato purée, and a little salt and pepper. Bring the pan to the boil, cover, and simmer for 1½–2 hours, until the beef and the beans are really tender. Taste and adjust the seasoning, if necessary.

4. For the garnish, top the tortillas with the cheddar cheese and put them under a hot broiler until the cheese has melted. Arrange 2 cheesy tortillas on top of each bowl of soup.

Opposite: Mexican Beef and Bean Soup.

CHAPTER SEVEN

CHILLED OUT

When the weather is too hot to cook and all you want to eat is subtly flavored cool food, start a meal with an indulgent iced soup or serve a chilled blend with freshly baked bread for a lazy lunch in the garden. Make sure that whatever you choose for your menu is really well chilled before serving. To keep a chilled soup's temperature down, float a couple of ice cubes in each bowl just before you set them on the table.

If the recipe includes stock, it must be as fat-free as possible, otherwise the soup will develop a greasy texture when it is chilled. If frying onions, garlic, or other vegetables before adding the stock and other ingredients, use oil rather than butter, and use as little as possible.

Most of the following recipes can be served hot, if preferred.

Chilled Yoghurt Soup

Serves 6

1 tablespoon rich fruity olive oil
1[?] teaspoon mustard seeds
2 ¾ cups thick plain Greek yoghurt
1 ¼ cups vegetable stock
½ cucumber, peeled and grated
2 garlic cloves, peeled and very finely chopped
finely grated rind of ½ lime
salt and freshly ground black pepper
2 tablespoons fresh chopped mint

1. Heat the light olive oil in a small pan and add the mustard seeds. Stir over a high heat until the seeds start to pop. Remove from the heat and cool.

2. Beat the yoghurt with a wooden spoon until smooth and creamy. Gradually add the stock and mix well.

3. Add the cucumber, garlic, lime rind and juice, salt and pepper, chopped mint, mustard seeds, and olive oil. Blend carefully, adjust the seasoning, if necessary, and chill.

4. Serve very cold, garnished with mint leaves.

Watercress and Apple Soup

The slight pepperiness of the watercress goes well with the apple in this soup, and provides plenty of iron and vitamins B and C.

Serves 6

1–2 tablespoons light olive oil
2 leeks, sliced
¾ lb potato, peeled and diced
3 bunches or bags of watercress
4 dessert apples, peeled, cored and chopped
1 ½ quarts chicken stock (see p.37)
   or vegetable stock (see p.41)
1 ¼ cups milk
salt and freshly ground black pepper
squeeze of fresh lemon juice

For the garnish:
light cream
sprigs of watercress

1. Heat the oil in a large saucepan. Add the leeks, cover the pan and sweat for 5 minutes, until the leeks are beginning to soften. Add the potato, cover the pan again and sweat for 3–4 minutes.

2. Add the watercress, apples, and stock to the pan, reduce the heat, cover, and simmer for 25–30 minutes.

3. Allow the mixture in the pan to cool, then purée it in a blender or food processor until very smooth. Transfer the purée to a large bowl and stir in the milk. Taste and adjust the seasoning, if necessary, then add a squeeze of lemon juice. Chill the soup for several hours before serving it.

4. Serve the soup garnished with a swirl of light cream and a sprig of watercress.

Opposite: Watercress and Apple Soup

Roasted Tomato and Basil Soup

Roasting the tomatoes in this soup before mixing them in brings out all their sweetness and flavor.

Serves 4

2lb tomatoes
olive oil, for brushing
2 teaspoons sugar
6–8 garlic cloves, skins left on
2 tablespoons olive oil
2 onions, peeled and chopped
1 quart chicken stock (see p.37) or
    vegetable stock (see p.41)
2–3 drops hot pepper sauce
large handful of fresh basil leaves,
    roughly torn into pieces
salt and freshly ground black pepper
sprigs of fresh basil, to garnish

1. Preheat the oven to gas 400°F/200°C. Cut the tomatoes in half and brush with a little olive oil. Place in a roasting pan, cut side uppermost, and sprinkle over the sugar. Brush the garlic cloves with a little olive oil and place on top of the tomatoes. Roast for 20–30 minutes, taking out the garlic earlier if it begins to dry and burn.

2. Allow the roasted tomatoes and garlic to cool a little. Squeeze the garlic flesh from its skin and mash. Scoop the tomato flesh and juice from the skins. Discard the skins.

3. Heat the 2 tablespoons of olive oil in a large saucepan. Add the onions and gently fry until soft and translucent. Add the roasted tomatoes and mashed garlic to the pan with the stock, hot pepper sauce, basil, and a little salt and pepper. Bring to the boil, reduce the heat, cover the pan, and simmer for 30 minutes.

4. Allow the soup to cool, then purée it in a blender or food processor. Taste and adjust the seasoning, if necessary. Chill for several hours before serving.

5. Serve the soup garnished with sprigs of fresh basil.

Carrot, Orange, and Tarragon Soup

This soup can be served hot on chilly days or chilled as a refreshing starter on steamy ones.

Serves 4–6

1–2 tablespoons olive oil
2 onions, peeled and roughly chopped
2 garlic cloves, peeled and chopped
2lb carrots, peeled and roughly chopped
1 quart chicken stock (see p.37) or
    vegetable stock (see p.41)
1 tablespoon fresh tarragon, chopped
salt and freshly ground black pepper
juice of 6 oranges

For the garnish:
²/₃ cup light cream
2 tablespoons Greek yoghurt
fine strips of orange zest

1. Heat the oil in a large saucepan. Add the onions, garlic, and carrots. Cover the pan and sweat the vegetables over a low heat for 5 minutes, being careful not to allow them to brown.

2. Add the stock, tarragon, and a little salt and pepper. Bring to the boil, reduce the heat, cover the pan, and simmer for 45 minutes, until the carrots are really soft.

3. Allow the mixture to cool, then purée it in a blender or food processor. Add the orange juice, and adjust the seasoning, if necessary. Chill for several hours.

4. To serve, mix together the light cream and the yoghurt and spoon a little into the middle of each bowlful of soup. Place a sprig of tarragon and a little orange zest on top.

Opposite: Roasted Tomato and Basil Soup.

Chilled Shrimp and Cucumber Cream

This is a true summer soup—light, subtle, fresh, and cooling.

Serves 4–6

3 cucumbers, peeled and roughly chopped
2 garlic cloves, peeled and chopped
1 quart chicken stock (see p.37) or
    fish stock (see p.40)
10oz peeled shrimp
2 tablespoons lime juice
salt and freshly ground black pepper
²/₃ cup Greek yoghurt
²/₃ cup light cream
slices of cucumber, to garnish

1. Put the cucumber into a food processor with the garlic and a little stock and purée until very smooth. Pour into a large bowl.

2. Reserve a few whole shrimp for garnishing and put the rest in the blender or food processor with a little more of the stock, the lime juice, salt and pepper, and yoghurt. Process together until smooth.

3. Add the shrimp purée to the bowl with the cucumber and the remaining stock. Stir in the cream, making sure the mixture is well blended. Adjust the seasoning, if necessary. Chill for several hours.

4. To serve, arrange a whole shrimp on top of a slice of cucumber and float one slice on each bowl of soup.

Left: Chilled Shrimp and Cucumber Cream.

Iced Avocado and Lemon Soup

Instead of blending the tomatoes into the avocado mixture they are chopped and spooned in as a salsa garnish just before serving.

Serves 4–6

4 ripe avocados
juice of 1 lemon
1 teaspoon grated fresh root ginger
1 quart vegetable stock (see p.41)
2–3 drops hot chili sauce
²⁄₃ cup light cream
salt and freshly ground black pepper
4 plum tomatoes
a few fresh basil leaves, finely shredded

1. Cut the avocados in half, remove the pit and scoop out the flesh into a food processor or blender. Add the lemon juice and ginger and purée until really smooth.

2. Turn into a bowl and mix in the vegetable stock, chili sauce, cream, and a little salt and pepper. Chill for several hours.

3. Meanwhile, soak the tomatoes in boiling water for 4–5 minutes until the skins come off easily. Cut away any hard core, squeeze away the seeds and chop the flesh into neat little cubes. Mix with the shredded basil leaves, a little salt and black pepper and chill.

4. To serve, ladle into bowls and spoon a little of the tomato and basil mixture into the middle of each.

Fennel and Roasted Red Pepper Soup

This vitamin-packed combination is rich in flavor and can be served hot or chilled.

Serves 6

1 red pepper, halved and deseeded
1–2 tablespoons olive oil
2 shallots, peeled and chopped
2 heads of fennel, thinly sliced
1³⁄₄ quarts chicken stock (see p.37)
   or vegetable stock (see p.41)
2 teaspoons chopped fresh marjoram
salt and freshly ground black pepper
sprigs of fresh dill, to garnish

1. Brush the red pepper halves with a little olive oil and broil, skin side up, until the skin is charred all over. Put in a plastic bag, allow to cool slightly and then pull away and discard the skin. Chop the flesh.

2. Heat the oil in a large saucepan. Add the shallots and gently fry until soft and translucent. Add the fennel and chopped red pepper, cover the pan and sweat the vegetables over a low heat for 10 minutes.

3. Add the stock, marjoram, and a little salt and pepper. Bring to the boil, reduce the heat, cover the pan, and simmer for 45 minutes.

4. Allow the mixture to cool, then purée in a blender or food processor. Pour into a large bowl, adjust the seasoning if necessary, and chill for several hours.

5. Serve the soup garnished with dill.

Opposite: Iced Avocado and Lemon Soup.

Sweet Potato, Chicken, and Toasted Sesame Seed Soup

Quite a filling mixture, this makes a great summer light meal or lunchtime hunger-stopper.

Serves 4-6

1 tablespoon sesame oil
1 tablespoon olive oil
2 shallots, peeled and chopped
2 chicken breast halves, trimmed of fat and sinew
2lb sweet potato flesh, chopped
$1\frac{1}{2}$ quarts chicken stock (see p.37)
1 teaspoon fresh thyme
salt and freshly ground black pepper
$1\frac{1}{4}$ cups milk
2–3 tablespoons toasted sesame seeds, to garnish

1. Heat the oils together in a large saucepan. Add the shallots and gently fry until soft and translucent.

2. Cut the chicken into small pieces. Add to the pan and stir-fry until sealed all over. Add the sweet potato, stock, thyme, and a little salt and pepper and bring to the boil. Cover the pan and simmer very gently for 45 minutes, until the chicken is really tender and the sweet potato is falling apart.

3. Allow the mixture to cool, then purée it in a blender or food processor until really smooth and creamy. Pour into a large bowl. Stir in the milk and taste and adjust the seasoning, if necessary. Chill for several hours.

4. Serve the soup topped with a sprinkling of toasted sesame seeds.

Left: Sweet Potato, Chicken, and Toasted Sesame Seed Soup.

Chilled Asparagus Soup

The luxury taste of fresh asparagus is wonderful blended into this cool, creamy soup.

Serves 6

1–2 tablespoons light olive oil
6 scallions, roughly chopped
2 garlic cloves, peeled and chopped
450g (1lb) asparagus spears, trimmed and
 cut into short pieces
1 cup diced potato
1¾ quarts chicken stock (see p.37) or
 vegetable stock (see p.41)
salt and freshly ground black pepper
curled strips of scallion or flat-leafed parsley,
 to garnish

1. Heat the oil in a large saucepan. Add the scallions and gently fry until soft and translucent. Add the garlic and cook gently for 2 minutes.

2. Add the asparagus, potato, stock, and a little salt and pepper. Bring to the boil, reduce the heat, cover the pan, and simmer for 20–25 minutes until the asparagus is tender.

3. Allow the mixture to cool, then purée it in a blender or food processor until very smooth. Pour the soup into a large bowl, adjust the seasoning, if necessary and chill for several hours.

4. Serve the soup garnished with curled strips of scallions (see p.120) or sprigs of flat-leafed parsley.

Chilled Celery and Beet Consommé

Beets are a good supply of natural sugars which provide energy. Its sweetness lends itself well to this clear, thin summer soup.

Serves 4

4 cooked beets, peeled and diced small
1 quart chicken stock (see p.37)
2 onions, peeled and chopped
6 sticks celery, chopped
a handful of fresh basil leaves
2–3 large sprigs fresh parsley
2-3 sprigs fresh thyme
a little salt
strip of lemon zest
6 black peppercorns
1 tablespoon lime juice
sprigs of fresh basil, to garnish

1. Put all the ingredients for the soup, except the lime juice, into a saucepan and bring to the boil. Reduce the heat, cover the pan, and simmer gently for 45 minutes, until all the vegetables are very soft.

2. Strain through a fine sieve, pressing the vegetables gently to extract as much liquid as possible without pushing any of the pulp through the mesh. Add the lime juice and adjust the seasoning, if necessary. Chill for several hours.

3. Serve the soup garnished with fresh basil leaves floating on top.

Opposite: Chilled Celery and Beet Consommé

CHAPTER EIGHT

BEARING FRUIT

Several recipes in previous chapters use fruit such as limes, lemons, and apples, but here I include more unusual and unexpected combinations to add exciting and exotic flavors and textures to more familiar soup ingredients. Some of the following recipes are for hot soups and others for chilled. There are also ideas for dessert "smoothies" that blend fruits with yoghurts, creams, and juices to make thick, filling, shake-like soups or desserts.

Turkey and Cranberry Soup

Dried and sweetened cranberries give a wonderful sweet-tart flavor to this turkey mixture. The cashew nuts are optional but delicious.

Serves 6

2–3 tablespoons olive oil
4 onions, peeled and sliced
4–5 turnips, peeled and cut into small cubes
2 carrots, scraped and cut into small cubes
½lb turkey fillet, trimmed of fat
    and cut into ¾-inch cubes
2 teaspoons dried or 1 tablespoon fresh sage
2 bay leaves
2¼ quarts chicken or turkey stock (see p.37)
1½ cup dried cranberries
salt and freshly ground black pepper
1 cup salted cashew nuts (optional)
beurre manié made from 3–4 tablespoons flour
    mixed with ¼ cup softened butter (see p.54)
fresh basil leaves or flat-leafed parsley, to garnish

1. Heat the oil in a large saucepan. Add the onions and gently fry until transparent and softened. Add the turnips and carrots, cover the pan, and sweat over a low heat for 5–6 minutes.

2. Add the turkey meat and cook on a high heat, turning the pieces until they are sealed all over.

3. Add the sage, bay leaves, stock, cranberries, and salt and pepper. Bring to the boil, reduce the heat, cover the pan, and simmer gently for 30 minutes, until the meat is tender.

4. Add the cashew nuts, if using, and simmer for a further 2 minutes. Taste and adjust the seasoning, if necessary. Add the *beurre manié* in small pieces to the mixture. Allow the soup to simmer until it has slightly thickened.

5. Serve the soup garnished with basil or flat-leafed parsley.

Lamb, Red Onion, and Mango Soup

Mango's exotically luxurious flavor goes really well with lamb, pork, or fish, and it adds a wonderful vibrant color to soups and stews.

Serves 6

2–3 tablespoons olive oil
3 red onions, peeled and thinly sliced
2 garlic cloves, peeled and finely chopped
1 red pepper, deseeded and cut into small cubes
1 green pepper, deseeded and cut into small cubes
1 teaspoon paprika
1½lb lamb, trimmed of fat and
    cut into small cubes
1¾ quarts chicken stock (see p.37)
    or lamb stock (see p.38)
juice of 2 limes
salt and freshly ground black pepper
2 mangoes, peeled and finely diced
2 tablespoons chopped fresh cilantro
beurre manié made from 3–4 tablespoons flour
    mixed with ¼ cup softened butter (see p.54)
sprigs of fresh cilantro, to garnish

1. Heat the oil in a large saucepan. Add the onions and gently fry until soft and translucent. Add the garlic, red and green peppers, and paprika. Cover the pan and sweat the vegetables over a low heat for 4–5 minutes.

2. Add the lamb and cook over a fairly high heat for a few minutes, turning the meat pieces until they are sealed all over.

3. Add the stock, lime juice, and a little salt and pepper. Bring to the boil, reduce the heat, cover the pan and simmer gently for 45 minutes to an hour, until the lamb is tender.

4. Add the mango and the cilantro to the pan and continue simmering for 15–20 minutes. Taste and adjust the seasoning, if necessary. Mix the *beurre manié* into the soup in small pieces. Allow to simmer until slightly thickened. Serve the soup garnished with cilantro.

Opposite: Turkey and Cranberrry Soup.

Overleaf: Lamb, Red Onion, and Mango Soup.

Tuna Soup with Orange and Avocado

Fresh tuna meat is easy to overcook and can sometimes be disappointingly dry and chewy, but in this juicy mixture it stays succulent and delicious.

Serves 6

2–3 tablespoons olive oil
2 onions, peeled, halved, and very thinly sliced
2 garlic cloves, peeled and finely chopped
1 teaspoon ground cumin
pinch of cinnamon
2 teaspoons chopped fresh parsley
finely grated zest and juice of 1 lime
²/₃ cup orange juice
1¼lb fresh tuna steaks,
    cut into ³/₄-inch cubes
1³/₄ quarts fish stock (see p.40)
salt and freshly ground black pepper
6 large tomatoes
4oz sugar snap peas or green beans,
    cut into short pieces
2 firm but ripe avocados, peeled, pitted
    and cut into neat cubes
sprigs of fresh flat-leafed parsley, to garnish

1. Heat the oil in a large saucepan. Add the onions and gently fry until soft and translucent. Add the garlic and gently fry for 2 minutes.

2. Add the cumin, cinnamon, parsley, lime zest and juice, orange juice, tuna, stock, and a little salt and pepper. Bring to the boil, reduce the heat, cover the pan, and simmer for 15 minutes.

3. Meanwhile, soak the tomatoes in boiling water for several minutes until the skin will peel easily away. Cut away the hard cores and chop the flesh. Add to the pan with the sugar snap peas or beans. Simmer for 4–5 minutes.

4. Just before serving the soup, stir the avocado cubes into the pan. Serve immediately, garnished with parsley.

Apricot and Apple Soup

This is an unusual combination and is great as a starter, either hot in winter or iced in summer.

Serves 6

1lb fresh apricots or ³/₄ lb
    ready-to-use dried apricots
1lb dessert apples, peeled, cored, and chopped
2 sticks celery, chopped
3–4 sprigs fresh parsley
1 bay leaf
1¹/₂ quarts very light chicken stock
    (see p.37) or vegetable stock (see p.41)
a little salt
juice of 1 lime
²/₃ cup heavy cream
¹/₂ cup toasted slivered almonds, to garnish

1. Put the apricots, apples, celery, parsley, bay leaf, and stock in a large saucepan and bring to the boil. Reduce the heat and simmer, covered, for about 30 minutes. Lift out the parsley and bay leaf with a slotted spoon and discard. Allow the mixture to cool a little.

2. Purée the mixture in a blender or food processor until smooth. Return to a clean saucepan, if the soup is to be served hot, or put in a large bowl. Add a little salt and the lime juice and stir in the cream.

3. To serve the soup hot, reheat it gently but do not allow it to boil. To serve it cold, chill for several hours and serve with 2–3 ice cubes floating in it. Toasted flaked almonds make a good garnish for the soup, either hot or cold.

Previous page: Tuna Soup with Orange and Avocado.

Opposite: Apple and Apricot Soup.

Cool Melon, Crab, and Ginger Soup

In this wonderful summer soup, the melon provides the perfect foil for the rich flavor of the crab meat. Serve this soup very cold.

Serves 6

2 ripe melons, such as galia, charentais, or honeydew
juice of 1 lime
1/2-inch piece of fresh root ginger, grated
1 quart fish stock (see p.40)
salt and freshly ground black pepper
10–12oz crab meat, drained if canned, and flaked
3–4 scallions, sliced diagonally, to garnish

1. Cut the melons in half and scoop out all the seeds. Scoop out the flesh, chop it roughly and put into a large saucepan with the lime juice, ginger, stock, salt, and pepper. Bring to the boil, reduce the heat, cover the pan, and simmer for 10–15 minutes. Allow the mixture to cool.

2. Put the mixture in a blender or food processor and process until very smooth. Transfer to a large bowl, stir in the flaked crab meat and chill for several hours.

3. Serve the soup garnished with the slices of scallion.

Mango, Papaya, and Passion Fruit Smoothie

Serve this thick creamy fruity mixture as a lunchtime snack or a cool dessert after a light meal.

Serves 4

2 mangoes, peeled and cut from the pit
2 papayas, peeled and seeds removed
juice of 1 lime
a little honey, to taste
4 tablespoons thick Greek yoghurt
4 passion fruit

For the decoration:
strawberry slices or fresh raspberries
sprigs of mint

1. Put the mango and papaya flesh in a blender or food processor. Add the lime juice, honey, and yoghurt and process until smooth.

2. Cut the passion fruit in half and scoop out the flesh and pips. In a bowl, stir the passion fruit into the yoghurt mixture, blend well and chill.

3. To serve, turn the soup into individual bowls or dishes and garnish each with a strawberry slice or a couple of fresh raspberries and a mint leaf.

Opposite: Cool Melon, Crab and Ginger Soup.

Cranberry, Apple, and Mint Soup

This makes an unusual, fresh starter or simply a quick refreshing snack in the middle of the day.

Serves 4

2$\frac{1}{4}$ cups cranberry juice
1$\frac{1}{2}$lb dessert apples, peeled, cored, and chopped
juice of 1 lemon
2–3 tablespoons sugar or honey, to taste
1 tablespoon fresh mint leaves
mint leaves, to garnish

1. Put the cranberry juice, apples, lemon juice, and sugar or honey in a large saucepan and bring to the boil. Reduce the heat, cover the pan, and simmer gently until the apples are soft. Allow the mixture to cool.

2. Transfer to a blender or food processor and process until smooth. Add the mint leaves and whiz for a few seconds.

3. Turn the soup into a large bowl and chill for several hours. Serve garnished with fresh mint leaves.

Chilled Cherry Soup

If you can bear not to simply tuck into the cherries as they are, turn them into this wonderful sweet soup and you will be glad you resisted.

Serves 4

1lb dark Morello cherries
1$\frac{1}{2}$ cups sweet white wine
$\frac{1}{4}$ cup sugar or honey
2 inch piece cinnamon stick
2 strips of lime zest
juice of 2 limes
$\frac{1}{3}$ cup brandy
1$\frac{1}{4}$ cups lightly whipped heavy
   cream, to garnish

1. Stone the cherries and reserve the flesh. Crack the cherry pits with a rolling pin and put into a saucepan with the wine, sugar or honey, cinnamon stick, and the lime zest and juice. Bring to the boil, reduce the heat, cover the pan, and simmer gently for 10 minutes.

2. Strain the juice into a clean pan, add the reserved cherries with any juice that has seeped out. Bring to the boil, reduce the heat, cover the pan, and simmer for 3–4 minutes. Allow to cool.

3. Transfer to a blender or food processor and process for just a few seconds, to break down the flesh but not completely pulverize it. Pour the mixture to a large bowl, stir in the brandy and chill for several hours.

4. Serve the soup in individual bowls with a generous dollop of lightly whipped cream in each.

Opposite: Cranberry, Apple, and Mint Soup.

FINAL
TOUCHES

Adding a garnish or decoration to soup—or, in fact, to any dish—makes a huge difference to the effect as it is placed on the table. There are no hard and fast rules about what to use as final touches, but keep them small, neat, and light— garnishes should enhance food, not hide or overwhelm it. Use whatever you have that is suitable for serving with particular flavors or ingredients, colors and textures.

Ideas for Garnishing Soups

Very effective garnishes can be achieved instantly simply by reaching for the nearest fresh herb. Others can be made almost as quickly by combining ingredients always to hand in the kitchen. Then there are others that need some advance planning, and even a bit of cooking. The ideas that follow include examples of all three.

- Swirl in a little heavy cream, half and half, sour cream, or crème fraîche.

- Mix a finely chopped fresh herb, suitable for the soup to be garnished, into thick Greek yoghurt and put a dollop on top of the soup. Good herbs for this include parsley, chives, mint, tarragon, chervil, and cilantro.

- Spoon in some plain yoghurt and sprinkle over it a finely chopped herb or a contrasting spice, such as paprika, black pepper, poppy seeds, or mustard seeds.

- Drop in a small spoonful of pesto. This is particularly good with vegetable soups.

- Sprinkle over a little grated cheese. Choose cheeses with good strong flavors, such as Cheddar, parmesan, or gruyère.

- Use sprigs of a suitable fresh herb—basil, mint, chervil, cilantro, flat-leafed parsley, sage, or thyme.

- Sprinkle over a few toasted almonds, chopped hazelnuts, chopped cashew nuts, or toasted sunflower, pumpkin, or sesame seeds.

- Scatter over a spoonful of very crispy crumbled bacon.

- Arrange a couple of deep-fried onion rings, parsley sprigs or cubes of tofu on the soup (see p.118).
- Using a zester, peel off very fine strips of lemon or lime zest and arrange them on top of swirls of cream or yoghurt.

- Drop in a few very neat julienne strips of blanched carrot, celery, scallion or slices of baby corn cut across the diagonal.

- Arrange a curled scallion or two on the soup (see p.120).

- Drop in a spoonful of saffron rice (see p.120).

- Add a few gnocchi or small dumplings (see p. 121).

- Spoon in a few croûtons (see p.123).

- Place one or two rounds of crostini, plain or topped with cheese, on the soup (see p.126).

- Arrange a few little diamonds or squares of herb omelet on the soup (see p.125).

Garnishes Made in the Kitchen

The garnishes that follow include ingredients that involve a bit of advance planning, as you may not have them to hand in the kitchen. Some also require cooking.

Opposite: Crispy bacon adds texture and an extra flavor to smooth soups.

Above: Fresh cilantro leaves.

Deep-fried Onion Rings, Parsley Sprigs, or Tofu Cubes

The amounts you will need of these ingredients depends on how many bowls of soup you wish to garnish.

1 onion, peeled and cut into rings ½-inch wide
fresh parsley sprigs, washed and dried
tofu, cut into ½–⅝ inch cubes

1. Pour olive oil into a heavy-based skillet to a depth of approximately 1 inch. Heat the oil until a small piece of onion or bread dropped into it sizzles immediately.

2. Carefully lower the ingredient to be fried (they should be fried separately) into the oil and fry until golden. Parsley needs only a few seconds. Lift out of the oil with a slotted spoon and drain on kitchen paper. Keep hot until needed.

Julienne Vegetable Strips

1. Scrub or peel a carrot (use a vegetable peeler to peel off as little skin as possible). Trim and scrub a stick of celery. Trim a couple of scallions.

2. With a sharp knife, cut the vegetables into fine strips approximately 1 inch long.

3. Bring water to the boil in a small saucepan. Drop in the vegetables. Allow to boil for 2 minutes then strain into a sieve and refresh under running cold water. Pat the vegetable strips dry on kitchen paper.

4. When using, make sure that each bowl of soup is garnished with a little of each vegetable so that the blend of colors is even.

Opposite: Neat strips of vegetable make an attractive garnish in clear and smooth soups.

Scallion Curls

Trim a few scallions. With a sharp knife, and working on a wooden chopping board, cut the upper leaves into strips so that they are still attached to the onion but splay out into narrow leaves. Place in a bowl of iced water and leave in the freezer for half an hour. The shredded leaves will curl up. Pat the curls dry on kitchen paper and use as soon as possible to garnish a soup.

Above: Scallions can be sliced
diagonally, chopped finely or curled in iced water.

Saffron Rice

1. Put a few strands of saffron into a pan of lightly salted cold water and bring to the boil. Add 1-2 tablespoons long-grain rice, bring back to the boil, and simmer partially covered, for 12–15 minutes, or until the rice is tender.

2. Drain the rice into a sieve and rinse with boiling water. Drain well.

Above: Saffron rice adds a sharp color to dark soups.

Gnocchi

Makes about 26 gnocchi 1-inch in diameter.

1lb floury potatoes, unpeeled
1 cup all-purpose flour
1 egg, lightly beaten
pinch of grated nutmeg
salt and freshly ground black pepper
a little olive oil

1. Boil the potatoes in lightly salted water in their skins until tender. Drain and cool. Peel off the skin and push the potato flesh through a mouli-legume on to a floured work surface.

2. Make a well in the center of the mound of potato and add the flour, egg, nutmeg, salt and pepper, and a little oil. Work with floured hands to mix the ingredients to a stiff, smooth dough. If too stiff, add a little more oil. Knead the dough well until smooth. Put the ball of dough into a bowl, cover, and leave to rest for 30 minutes.

3. Bring a large saucepan of water to the boil.

4. On a lightly floured surface, roll out the dough to a long sausage and cut it into equal-sized lumps—you should get about 26. Roll each out to an oval or round.

5. Drop the gnocchi into the boiling water and poach for 5 minutes, until they pop up to the surface. As they come to the surface, scoop them out with a slotted spoon and drain them. Spoon the gnocchi into the pan of hot soup just before serving to allow them to warm through.

• To make **herb gnocchi**, add a tablespoon of chopped mixed herbs to the mixture when kneading.

Herb Dumplings

Makes 20 x 1-inch dumplings

$^2/_3$ cup all-purpose flour
1 teaspoon baking powder
teaspoon salt
1 egg
$^1/_3$ cup milk
2 tablespoons chopped mixed chopped herbs,
    such as basil, thyme, parsley, and marjoram
a little grated lemon zest

1. Sift together the flour, baking powder, and salt into a bowl. Make a well in the middle. Beat the egg and milk together lightly and pour into the well. Mix to make a stiff dough, adding a little more milk if it is too stiff.

2. Drop small spoonfuls of the dough into the simmering soup, cover the saucepan and allow the dumplings to cook for 10 minutes.

• To make **cheese dumplings**, mix $^1/_4 - ^1/_2$ cup grated mature Cheddar cheese into the mixture instead of the herbs. For **herb and cheese dumplings**, leave the herbs in and add the cheese as well.

Plain Croûtons

Enough to garnish 6 servings

6 slices day-old bread
3–4 tablespoons olive oil
a little salt and freshly ground black pepper

1. Preheat the oven to 350°F/180°C. Cut the crusts from the bread. Using mini pastry or biscuit cutters, cut the bread into cubes, triangles, diamonds, stars, crescents or other shapes.

2. Pour the olive oil into a bowl and add salt and pepper. Toss the bread in the oil until it has all been absorbed.

3. Put the pieces of bread in a single layer on a baking sheet. Bake in the oven for 10–15 minutes, until golden and crisp. Turn the bread shapes once or twice during the cooking time so that they become golden all over.

- To make **herb croûtons**, add 1 tablespoon chopped fresh parsley, 1 tablespoon fresh thyme leaves, or 1 tablespoon chopped fresh marjoram or oregano to the oil before tossing the bread in it. Bake as above.

- To make **garlic croûtons**, add 2–3 chopped garlic cloves to the oil before tossing the bread in it. Bake as above.

- To make **parmesan croûtons**, mix 55g (2oz) finely grated parmesan cheese to the oil before tossing the bread in it. Make sure that all the pieces of bread are coated with the cheese.

- To make **pesto croûtons**, before cutting the bread slices into shapes, spread both sides with a thin layer of pesto.

Blue Cheese Croûtons

Enough to garnish 4 servings

4 slices day-old bread
25g (1oz) butter, softened
85g (3oz) creamy blue cheese
a few chives, snipped small

1. Cut the crusts from the bread and toast it very lightly.

2. Mix the butter with the blue cheese and snipped chives. Spread the mixture on to the toast and place under a moderate grill until the cheese begins to bubble.

3. Cut the cheese croûtons into squares, strips or triangles and immediately float on the top of the soup.

Opposite: Fresh crusty bread is the perfect accompaniment to any soup.
Right: Croutons—a simple but always effective garnish for soups.

Garlic Crostini

Enough to garnish 4 servings

4 garlic cloves, skins left on
3–4 tablespoons olive oil
pinch of salt and freshly ground black pepper
half a stick of French bread

1. Preheat the oven to 350°F/180° C. Brush the garlic cloves with a little oil, spread on a baking tray and cook in the oven for 10–15 minutes.

2. Allow the garlic cloves to cool a little, then squeeze the flesh from the skins and mash together with the olive oil and a little salt.

3. Cut the bread into 8 slices and spread some of the garlic and oil mixture on to one side of each slice.

4. Put the slices of bread on a baking tray and bake in the oven for 8–10 minutes until golden. Put two crostini on top of each serving of soup.

- To make **cheese-topped crostini**, top the baked garlic crostini with grated Cheddar, gruyère, Swiss, or a similar cheese and flash under the broiler until the cheese starts to melt.

- To make **béchamel- and cheese-topped crostini**, make a thick béchamel sauce with 2 tablespoons butter blended with 2 tablespoons flour and approximately $^2/_3$ cup milk. Lightly toast the slices of French bread, spread with the cooked, thickened sauce, top with grated cheese and bake in the oven for 10 minutes until golden.

- To make **herb crostini**, make as for garlic crostini, adding fresh chopped herbs, such as tarragon, marjoram, thyme, or chives, to the oil and garlic. Omit the garlic, if you prefer.

Herb Omelette

Makes a garnish for 4 bowls of soup

2 eggs
a little salt and freshly ground black pepper
1 teaspoon chopped fresh marjoram or oregano
1 teaspoon fresh thyme leaves
2 tablespoons butter or 1 tablespoon light olive oil

1. Beat the eggs with the salt, pepper, and herbs.

2. Heat the butter or oil in a non-stick omelette plan or small skillet and pour in the eggs. Cook gently until the eggs are set and lightly browned on the underside. Flip the omelet over and very lightly brown it on the other side.

3. Slide the omelette out of the pan and cut it into little squares, diamonds, rectangles, or triangles. Use immediately, or reheat in the microwave before adding to the bowls of soup.

Opposite: Garlic Crostini.

INDEX

Page numbers in *italic* refer
to the illustrations

PICTURE ACKNOWLEDGEMENTS

AKG, London 12r, 13/Musees Royaux d'Art et
d'Histoire, Brussels 10
Anthony Blake Photo Library 32, 92/T. Wood 39
Bridgeman Art Library, London/ British Library,
London, Duke of Lancaster dines with the king of
Portugal, from Vol.III 'From the Coronation of Richard
II to 1387', by Jean de Batard Wavrin Chronique
d'Angleterre (15th Century) 14/5,Lords Gallery,
London, Advertisement for Fuller's Clam Broth by
W.Henry Walker (b.1871) 17, Museo Archeologico
Nazionale, Naples, Italy, Red-figure bell krater depicting
a banquet scene (pottery) 12l, Barbara Singer,
Advertisement for 'L'Excellent Beef Consomme' (colour
litho) by French School (19th Century) 46
Corbis 6, 8, 9b
Mary Evans Picture Library 16
Food Features 21, 25l, 26, 30, 35, 36, 40
Robert Harding Picture Library 29/Fabbri 120l, S.
Hedderwick 27r, The Picture Store 25r, G. Stratton 9t
Courtesy Kenwood Limited. 28r
Courtesy Philips 28l
Howard Shooter/Carlton Books Ltd. 1, 2, 4, 7, 11, 19,
20, 22-24, 27l, 33r, 41-45, 48-91, 94-119, 120r, 122-4
Tony Stone Images/L. Dutton 18